The Joy of Marketing

Jokes and Anecdotes

from

Around the World

The Joy of Marketing

Jokes and Anecdotes

from

Around the World

Michal (Mickie) Gerstner
and
Eitan Gerstner

Illustrations by

Allon Gostiaux
Sean Huang

This book can be ordered through:
UCD Book Store
University of California
Davis, California 95616
Tel: (916) 752-2944
Fax: (916) 752-4791

Library of Congress Cataloging-in-Publication Data

Gerstner Michal (Mickie)
    The Joy of Marketing:
    Jokes and Anecdotes from Around the World/
    Michal(Mickie) Gerstner, Eitan Gerstner

ISBN 0-9643067-0-0
Library of Congress Catalog Number 94-96422

Cover design by Andy Markley, Camino, California
Front cover photo by Zeev Ramiel, Rehovot, Israel
Authors photo by Erron Evans, Davis, California
Photo on front cover: Armando Bismut, comedian, Mishmeret, Israel

To the memory of
our mothers
Eva Bauch
Shoshana Gerstner

Contents

Our Thanks

We have many to thank for their effort in making this book possible.

To Professor Jim Hess ("Singin' Jimmie") from the University of Illinois (Champaign, IL) for his insightful suggestions and comments.

To Professor Michael Hagerty (UC Davis, CA) for his good suggestion.

To Cindi Rich (UC Davis, CA), for her good advice.

To Ann Philips (Raleigh, NC) and James Emery (Davis, CA) for their help in editing the manuscript.

To Allon Gostiaux (Herzliya, Israel) and Sean Huang (Davis, CA) for their beautiful illustrations.

To Andy Markley (Sacramento, CA) who designed the cover of this book.

To Armando Bismut (Mishmeret, Israel) who gave us permission to use his photo on the cover, and to Zeev Ramiel (Rehovot, Israel) who took this photo.

To Erron Evans (Davis, CA) who took our photo on the back of the cover.

Thank you all!

Preface

Marketers help design new products, bring them to market at the right time and place, at the right price, and convince customers to buy. They must develop good communication skills and abilities to understand people with different cultural backgrounds.

Bringing humor to marketing is a good way to relieve possible tensions and improve relationships between the parties involved. Humor can also increase attention, enhance memory, and help obtain good response from consumers. Needless to say, humor can improve the teaching and learning of marketing and make it more enjoyable.

To our surprise, we could not find any books that focus on marketing humor. Our objective is to fill this gap. This book offers a collection of jokes and anecdotes classified according to the marketing process described in a standard marketing textbook. For example, you will find jokes on the 4 P's of marketing (i.e., Product, Place, Pricing and Promotion).

Each chapter starts with a brief description of the marketing topic and the typical issues involved. The jokes and anecdotes that follow relate to the issues. They were collected, edited and adapted from wit and humor books written in English, French, Spanish, Yiddish, Arabic, German, Hebrew and more.

We hope that this collection will be useful to marketing educators, students, practitioners, and others who believe in the usefulness of applying humor to business. So read the jokes, enjoy them, pass them along, and remember what Oscar Wilde said: "Seriousness is the only refuge of the shallow."

Humor and Lore

In this book you will discover that humor travels well across cultures. Here is a description of some of the folk heros mentioned in the jokes:

Gabrovo is a town in Bulgaria. You will laugh at the Gabrovonians, but they, in fact, view themselves as being more sensible and serious than we. Don't call these thrifty people misers ...

Who is Mulla Nasrudin? "Mulla" is from the Arabic. It is a title of respect given to a religious Muslim sage. Turks as well as Greeks regard Mulla Nasrudin as part of their folklore. More recently he became a people's hero of the Russians. He shades off into the Arab figure of Juha, and re-appears in the folklore of Sicily.

"Juha stories" are known throughout the Arab world as well as in Turkey and Iran. They combine humorous simplicity with a kind of "illogical logic."

Chelm, the Polish town, is not fictional. It is about two-hundred kilometers south-east of Warsaw! It became a symbol of the "fools' town" in Eastern European Jewish folklore. Many writers, speakers and teachers have used a Chelm joke or anecdote to illustrate and make a point, adapting and tailoring it to their specific needs. In most cases, the stories present a problem to which the "Chelm Sages" suggest a logical solution that is not very practical...

Finally, Hershele the Ostropoler is a character used in East European jewish jokes. His name is based on the small town of Ostropol in Poland. According to legend, Hershele lost his job because of his constant joking, which was offensive to the leaders of the community. After a lot of wandering, he eventually arrived at his calling at the court of a rabbi who was plagued by frequent depressions - and served as kind of court jester.

1. What Is Marketing?

When asked what is marketing, many say it involves selling or advertising. This is only part of the answer. Marketing also includes decisions about products and services, distribution and pricing, leading to exchanges that meet the objectives of buyers and sellers. Marketers encourage exchanges by making products and services available in the right place and time. Other marketing activities illustrated below are: matching buyers and sellers, financing, marketing research, and reducing business risk.

Marketing Involves Exchanges

A Mutual Beneficial Exchange (Bulgaria)

One day Pencho was visiting Gabrovo. He took out his matches to light a cigarette.

"Don't bother yourself," a passer-by stopped Pencho, offering him his cigarette for a light.

Pencho accepted the light.

"And now," said the Gabrovonian smiling, "can you give me your match?"

Exchange.

Exchanging Smell for Sound (China)

A very poor Chinese operated a small laundry next door to a more prosperous Chinese restaurant. Every day he took his simple bowl of rice, placed his chair as near as he dared to the restaurant, and sniffed the appetizing aromas as he ate.

One day, the poor Chinese received a bill from his neighbor "for the smell of food." He went into his laundry and came out with his tiny money box. He rattled it in the ears of his creditor, saying:
"I hereby pay for the smell of your food with the sound of my money!"

Matching Products to Customers is Not Easy

Matching Music to the Ears of the Ox (China)

One day Kung Ming Yi, the celebrated musician, was playing an elegant tune on his harp to amuse a browsing ox. The ox, however, continued to munch, paying no heed to him at all.

Then he struck up some different notes, which sounded like mosquitoes droning and calves bleating. With this, the ox flicked its tail, pricked up its ears, and began frisking round and round, evidently absorbed in the music.

Get That Rembrandt Fellow (Israel)

A work-organizer at an Israeli kibbutz asked a Dutch volunteer:

"Do you know how to paint?"

"Not as professional as Rembrandt, but I can paint a barn," answered the volunteer.

The work-organizer paused for a moment to think, then said:

"Listen, I want this to be as professional as possible. Go back to the volunteers' quarters and see if that Rembrandt fellow can come and paint the barn."

Matchmaking Fee (Poland)

As soon as the morning service was over in the synagogue, Isaac Dreyer, the matchmaker, ran over to the wealthy Reb Hayim Nagid.

"Reb Hayim," said Isaac, "let me give you a hearty mazel tov on your daughter's marriage. By right, I'm entitled to the regular matchmaker's fee."

"How come?" asked Hayim, "you never told me anything about this match."

"That's just why I am entitled to a fee," said Isaac. "If I had spoken to you, the match would never have materialized!"

Matching Customer to Product (Arabic)

A middle-aged man had two wives. One was young and the other old. The young wife wanted him to look younger, so she used to pull his white hair out. The older wife wanted him to look older, so she pulled his dark hair out. Both women reached full satisfaction only when the man became bald... .

Mismatchmaking (Poland)

Zelda, the wife of Isaac the matchmaker, was complaining to her friends:
"My husband is a perfect good-for-nothing. The other day, for example, he told me that he brought together two of the wealthiest families in Poland. However, when the parents of the future couple met, it was discovered that both of them had daughters..."

Marketing Can Be Risky

"Like Juha's Trading in Eggs" (Egypt)

One day Juha thought he would set up in business, and decided to trade in eggs. So he opened a shop, bought a consignment of eggs, and started selling them. His principal concern, however, was to maximize sales, regardless of whether he made any profit. Since most of the time he sold his eggs cheaper than he bought them, he soon lost both his capital and his eggs, and became bankrupt.

The expression "Like Juha's trading in eggs" has since become a popular Arab saying, used to describe a commercial venture that fails by reason of the incompetence or inexperience of the person undertaking it.

Take-Out or Stakeout

Holdup man to cashier in a Chinese restaurant: "Give me all your money!"
Cashier: "To take out?"

Trading with a Snake (Arabic fable)

One day a farmer saw a snake in the field. He grasped him by his throat and wanted to cut his head off with a knife.

"If you let me live," pleaded the snake, "I will give you every day one gold dinar."

"And how do I know," asked the farmer, "that what you are saying is true? Let's make a contract!"

They signed a contract, and every morning from then on the farmer went to the snake's pit and found a golden dinar there. One morning when he took his dinar, the snake bit his hand.

"Didn't we sign a contract?" asked the farmer, in utter shock.

"Next time," answered the snake, looking straight into the farmer's eyes, "don't sign a contract with a snake!"

The Rabbi's New Ruling

In the marketplace, Ruben was telling the news to a big crowd of shoppers.

"You know," he said, very excitedly, "the rabbi has just ruled that no women may show up in front of the stock exchange building between twelve noon and one o'clock!"

"Why? What's the reason for that?" several people asked, astonished.

"At this time," said Ruben, "many a men leave the building with no pants on!"

8

Insurance and Semantics

"What would I get," inquired the store owner who had just insured his property against fire, "if this building should burn down tonight?"
"I would say about ten years," replied the insurance agent.

Planning Shortages (Czechoslovakia)

"Marketing in our place is meticulously planned," said a Czech homemaker, "every time when there is a shortage in bacon, there's a shortage in eggs."

Is There Anything For Sale Here? (Russia)

After waiting in line in front of a "people's store" for a long time, a Moscovite finally reached the counter.
"Do you have any coats?"
"Sorry, there aren't any," replied the clerk.
"How about shirts, do you have any?"
"We're out of shirts, too."
"Then do you have any socks left? I need some badly."
"They're all gone too," shouted the clerk, "and don't bother me. This is a store, not an information bureau!"

Marketing People Must Have the Right Skills

Always Be Patient (China)

A clerk was promoted to a marketing position. A close friend came to congratulate him.
"One thing you must remember," he said. "In dealing with people, always be patient."
The man replied that he would. His friend then repeated his advice three times, and three times the man nodded in agreement. When for the fourth time his friend repeated his counsel, the man became angry.
"Do you take me for an idiot? Why do you repeat such a simple thing over and over again?"
"See," said the friend, "I have only said that a few times, and you are already impatient!"

Marketing Jobs with Potential

A Job with Vision

An applicant was interviewed for a marketing position.
"What we are looking for," said the personnel manager, "is a man of vision, a man with drive, determination and courage, a man who never quits, who can inspire others, in short - a man who can pull the company's bowling team out of last place."

Moving to Winnipeg

A guy wanted to buy half a cabbage. The clerk in the supermarket went to see the manager and said:
"I have here an idiot who wants half a cabbage!"
He did not notice that the customer followed him to the manager's office. When he did notice him, he continued:
"... but this nice guy wants to buy the second half!"
The manager was very impressed and pleased with the way the clerk handled this incident, and offered him to manage the company's supermarket in Winnipeg.
"Winnipeg?" retorted the clerk, "there are only hookers and hockey players in Winnipeg!"
"What do you mean?" said the manager, "my mom is from there!"
"Really?" asked the clerk, "what team did she play for?"

Vice-President Marketing

Jack came home extremely happy and told his wife he had been promoted to Vice-President of Marketing for his company.
"Big deal," said his wife nonchalantly. "In our supermarket we have lots of vice-presidents. We even have a vice-president in the prunes department!"
"That's impossible!" said Jack.
"You don't believe it? Call them and hear it for yourself!"
And so he did:
"May I please speak with the vice-president of the prunes department?"
"Bulk or packaged?" asked the person at the other end.

Marketing Requires Trust

Exchange and Security (American Indians)

A Cherokee Chief asked a bank for a $300 loan.
"What security have you got?" asked the loan officer.
"I've got three hundred horses." This was satisfactory, so the loan was granted.

Several weeks later the Chief entered the bank, pulled out a huge roll of bills, counted off the $300 he owed, added interest, and started to leave.
"Wait," said the loan officer, "I see you've got a lot of money. Why don't you let us take care of it for you?"
"How many horses you got?" asked the Indian.

Finding a Marketing Job

A Marketing Job (Old Russia)

Victor was out of work. Desperately needing a job, he went to the employment agency. He entered the office, and saw two doors. On one of them a sign said, "married." On the other one; "single." Being unmarried, he used the second door and entered the second room.

In that room there were also two doors. The sign on one said, "party members" and on the other, "others." He used the first door and entered a third office. Again he saw two doors. One of them had a sign that said, "manufacturing." The other door said, "marketing." He used the second door and found himself back in the street!

Sometimes Marketing
Involves Conflict

Violins, Trumpets, and Guns

A pawnbroker loaded his show window with violins, trumpets, trombones, tubas - and shotguns.

"Very interesting display," commented a friend, "but does it sell merchandise?"

"Does it!" replied the pawnbroker. "One day a fellow buys a trumpet, another day his brother buys a trombone, and two days later their neighbors buy shotguns!"

Selling a Shadow (Arabic fable)

Juha sold his donkey to a neighbor. The next day he saw him sitting in the shadow of his donkey in the middle of the field. That day the sun was very strong in the sky. Said Juha:

"Get up and let me sit. I sold you the donkey but not its shadow!" They started to fight.

"The owner of the donkey," said the buyer, "is the owner of its shadow."

"No, man," said Juha, "you're very mistaken. The donkey is yours but the shadow is mine. You did not pay for it even one dinar."

The fight between the two men got out of hand, and when they started pushing and hitting each other, the donkey got real scared, and ran away from them, shadow and all...

2. The Marketing Environment

Marketing planning starts with a situation analysis in which a firm uses marketing research to become familiar with the marketing environment which includes the "three C's": Company, Consumers, and Competition. This research is used to assess opportunities and threats the firm may face.

Marketing Research
Helps Discover Opportunities

Computerized Information

A man met a young lady for the first time at a cocktail party. At his urging she later went to dinner with him and after that, dancing. He then took her home at 1:00 a.m. and asked her to marry him.

"But we only met a few hours ago. You don't know anything about me."

"Oh, yes I do," he said. "I work in the computer department of the bank where your father has his bank account."

Face to Face Interview (Poland)

A foreign marketing researcher interviewed a worker in Gdansk.

"Are you happy with your job?"

"Yes sir, very happy."

"And how is your apartment?"

"Modern, spacious and cheap."

"And what do you do for recreation?"

"I go to the opera and to the theater."

"Do you own a radio?"

"Sure I do. How do you think I learned to answer your stupid questions?"

A Survey (Spain)

A Marketing Research Consultant interviews a farmer in a small village in Spain:
"How many liters of milk do the cows give?"
"Which one, the white or the black cow?"
"The white one."
"Twelve."
"And the black one?"
"Also."
"What do the cows eat?"
"Which one, the white or the black one?"
"The white one."
"She eats alfalfa."
"And the black one?"
"Also."
The interviewer, a little perplexed, asked:
"If everything is the same for the two cows, why do you keep on asking me if I refer to the white cow or to the black cow?"
"Because the white cow is mine."
"And the black cow?"
"Also."

What Do They Buy?

Mark Twain tells: Once I was invited to lecture in a town named Squash, in the city hall. Arriving there I noticed there was no advertising for the lecture. I decided to check if anybody knew anything about it at all. I went into the local grocery store.

"Good evening sir," I greeted the owner. "Tell me, is there any entertainment tonight for a tourist like me?"

"Entertainment, no;" replied the grocer, wiping his hands in his apron. "But I think there is some lecture tonight, because all day long people were buying eggs and tomatoes."

Predicting Demand

Trading Cattle (Russia)

A group of Russian cattle dealers were returning from the monthly fair in the big city. On their way home they stopped at an inn and discussed their respective deals. None of them had made any sales.

One of the merchants commented:

"The cattle market was the worst I've ever seen. If not for me, there wouldn't have been a single decent ox."

Getting All the Facts Right

A Marketing Research Assistant presented to the president of his company a rosy sales forecast. After he finished, the president commented:
"Let me make a point by telling you this story:
The farmer's young son came rushing up to his father. 'Pa,' the boy said, 'come quick. Sis and the hired hand are up in the hayloft. She's got her skirt hiked up and he's got his pants down. I think they are going to pee all over our hay.'
'Son,' the farmer said calmly, 'I think you've got your facts right, but I'm afraid you've jumped to the wrong conclusion...'"

Legal Aspects of Marketing

The Shoemaker and the Carpenters (Arabic fable)

One day the village shoemaker was seen stealing from a neighbor's house. They took him to the mu'khtar (the head of the village). He grabbed him by his hair and brought him before Karakash the judge. The judge listened to the witnesses, and without questioning the shoemaker he said: "Hang him now!"
"Your honor," said the mu'khtar, "it's a shame to hang him. We have only one shoemaker in our village!"
"And carpenters, do we have?"
"Yes; two," said the mu'khtar.
"Hang one!" said Karakash the judge.

3. The Company

A marketing plan must take into account company resources such as personnel, capital, technological capabilities and know-how to assess its' strengths and weaknesses.

Successful Marketing Requires Planning

A Marketing Plan (Egypt)

There once was a righteous man who dedicated himself to the worship of God. And there was in town a kind-hearted merchant who used to send him oil and honey to help with his daily needs. The righteous man used to eat as much as he needed everyday, and store the leftovers in a jar, which he placed on a hook on the wall.

One hot day the righteous man was laying on his back, his stick in his hand, and the jug hanging in front of him. While contemplating, he had an idea: why not sell the oil and honey jug for a dinar? With it I will buy five goats. The goats will multiply and have babies. I'll sell them after a while and buy cows. Then, I'll sell milk and its products and after a while I'll use this money to buy some land, and hire farmers to toil it. By then I'll have lots of property and I'll buy slaves and marry a beautiful rich young lady. She will give birth to a handsome and talented boy and I'll give him the best education possible and treat him in a very strict way. If he stumbled on his way I would hit him with this stick like - so! -- And thinking about it he waved his stick, hit the jug, broke it, and the oil and honey spilled on his face ...

Organization Culture
Influences Marketing

Let's Get Started

After two years in the Pittsburgh office of a big organization, a beautiful Marketing Assistant was transferred to the New York headquarters.

The morning she reported to her new post, the Vice President Marketing called her into his inner sanctum. "I hope you'll be happy here. The work will be practically the same as you were doing in the Pittsburgh office." "Okay," she replied. "Kiss me, and let's get started!"

Marketers Must Find Opportunities

Market Is Wide Open

An American and a British shoe salesmen traveled on the same boat to West Africa, each representing different shoe companies. After landing, they looked around, and what struck them first was the fact that all the natives were barefoot.

The British chap cabled his head office: "Nobody here wearing shoes. Coming home by next ship."

The American salesman cabled his chief: "Nobody here wearing shoes. Market is wide open."

Big Opportunities in the Fish Market

Joe used to spend his days on the beach. When he got hungry, he used to catch one fish, cook it and eat it.
"Why don't you get a net?" people approached him, "you would catch ten fish, instead of just one!"
"Oh yeah? And what would I do with them?"
"Sell them and make money!"
"And what would I do with the money?"
"You can buy a boat and get more people and together you'll use lots of nets, get lots of fish, and one day you'll have lots of money!"
"And what would I do with that much money?"
"You'll be able to relax, sit on the beach, and have wonderful and careless life!"
"But I'm already doing it right now!" replied Joe, perplexed...

Marketers Must Reach Sales Goals

Creative Marketing

The boss and his sales manager looked gloomily at the sales chart on the wall. In one corner was a graph showing the company's descending grosses. The rest of the chart was a map of the territory, with pins stuck in to show the location of the various salesmen.

"Frankly," the boss sighed, "I think we have only one hope. Let's take the pins out of the map and stick them in the salesmen' behinds!"

4. Competitive Analysis

To keep customers coming, a company must provide products that match customers' needs better than the competitors', and at better prices. To compete successfully a company must learn the strengths and weaknesses of its competitors.

Some Companies Form Alliance to Limit Competition

Limiting Competition (Russia)

Hershele opened a fish restaurant and business was good. An old friend heard about it and stopped by.

"It's so good to see you, Hershele! Can you lend me five rubles?"

"I would lend you money, but I really can't. You see, I've signed a contract with the bank next door. They are not going to sell fish, and I'm not going to lend money!"

Cut-Throat Competition

A peddler advertised his cheap stationery in a loud voice, but nobody seemed to want a "box of fifty envelopes for twenty-five cents." Suddenly, however, another peddler arrived and began shouting:

"Here y'are folks! Box of fifty envelopes fer ten cents - one dime! Don't pay more!"

The two men glared at each other. A crowd gathered first to watch and then to buy out the complete stock of the merchant offering the ten-cent bargain. All the neighborhood bought enough envelopes to last the next five years.

A reporter followed the "quarter man" when he wheeled his cart away. Two blocks down, he caught up with the "ten-cent" peddler. The two men shook hands gleefully and started dividing up the "quarter man's" inventory.

Why Go Anywhere Else?

A woman brought a pair of shoes to a Nordstrom store.
"I bought them at Bloomingdale's," she said, "but they are too small. They were out of my size. Do you carry it?"
The salesperson found the right shoes and offered to replace them with the pair she brought in. The lady said: "But I bought them at Bloomingdale's!"
"That's all right. This way you will not have any reason to go back there ..."

A Smart Competitor Knows
When to Cut Price

Cut-Throat Competition

Mrs. Zilberknack entered Fleishaker's butchery.
"How much a pound for the lamb chops?" she asked.
"$1.45 a pound," answered Solomon Fleishaker.
"$1.45 a pound?! Across the street I can get lamb chops for $1.10 a pound!"
"Then why don't you buy them across the street?"
"They're all out of lamb chops."
"When I'm all out," said Fleishhaker the butcher, "they are only 97 cents a pound!"

Countering a Price Cut

On Lexington Street two vacuum-cleaner dealers were located next to each other. One day Jones decided to cut his vacuum cleaner prices from $70 to $50 a piece. The day of the sale a big sign went up in the window of his competitor: "WE REPAIR $50 VACUUM CLEANERS."

Sellers Watch Their Competitors

A Sign War

Two stores were engaged in bitter competition. Things reached a climax when one store flashed a notice saying: IF YOU NEED IT, WE HAVE IT. Whereupon the store across the street retorted: IF WE DON'T HAVE IT, YOU DON'T NEED IT.

Worrying About the Competition (Chelm, Poland)

The people of Chelm decided to build and run a mill. Since then they worried about everything: customers, competitors, profits, and more. To alleviate the situation, the Board of Trustees called a meeting of all the townsfolk.

A motion was made and duly seconded that Saul, the town shikker (drunkard) be retained to do all the worrying for Chelm and be paid one zloty per week for his trouble.

A wave of rejoicing greeted this wise solution until the Chairman of the Board asked a question that silenced the crowd:

"If the shikker is given a zloty every week," he demanded, "tell me, what will he have to worry about?"

5. Consumer Behavior

Information on consumers' tastes and purchase decisions is used to segment the market and focus effort on profitable target markets.

Consumers Want to Save Money

A Thoughtful Gift

Looking for an inexpensive gift for a friend, a penny pincher went into a gift shop but found everything too expensive.

Finally he saw a broken glass vase and found that he could buy it for almost nothing. He asked the store to ship it, hoping that his friend would think it had been broken in the mail.

After a while he received from his friend the following note: "Thank you for the vase. It was so thoughtful of you to wrap each piece separately."

How Much to Offer (Russia)

Sasha entered a clothing store, picked up a nice looking sweater, and asked:
"How much is it?"
"Twenty five rubles, sir."

Hearing this, Sasha began doing some calculations: Well, since he tells me twenty five, what he really means is twenty. Actually, the price for this sweater is fifteen. Which means I need to deduct five, and offer him five rubles!

Saving on Transportation (France)

One day little Paul returned home very content, and said to his father:
"Papa, I saved five francs today!"
"Oh, yes? And how did you do it?"
"I ran after the bus all the way home instead of riding it!"
"You little fool," said the father, "you could have run after a taxi and saved ten ..."

Marketers Need
to Respect Customers

A Gorgeous Stamp

A young man stood in the post office, waiting patiently while two clerks were busy talking.
"Her evening gown," said one of the girls, "had a metallic tone, she had a huge cut with a ribbon at the bottom, and the sleeves were full and fluffy."

When the girl stopped her description for a second in order to inhale, the young man managed to quickly say a few words:
"Excuse me, lady. Can you sell me a gorgeous stamp, pink in color, black at the perforated edges, smeared on its back with a sticky smelly liquid, for five cents?"

Looking for a Pen

Customer: "Do you keep fountain pens here?"
Store owner: "No, we sell them."
Customer: "Well, keep the one you might have sold me if you hadn't been so smart."

The Wine Expert

A famous wine taster got into a bar and asked for a bottle of Chambertain 1955. The barman went down to the basement and returned with a bottle. The man tasted and said:
"I've asked for 1955, not for 1956!"

The barman went again to the basement and brought a different bottle. The man tasted and said:
"I don't want 1954. I want 1955!"

The barman went down for the third time and brought yet a different bottle.
The expert took a sip and immediately spit the drink, an expression of sheer disgust on his face.
"It tastes like urine!" he said.
"That's true," replied the barman. "But of what year?"

Fast Service

"Are you the waiter who took my order?"
"Yes, Sir."
"You still look wonderful! And how are your grandchildren?"

Comparative Shopping

An old lady stepped up to the ticket window in the railway station and asked:
"How much is a ticket to Cleveland?"
"Ten dollars and seventy-nine cents," replied the agent.
    The lady turned to the little girl beside her and said:
"I guess we may as well buy our tickets here. I've asked at all those other windows, and been told the same price."

Bad Service (Egypt)

A man had pain in his eyes. To save money he went to see a vet. The vet put into his eyes the same medicine he used in treating animals, and the patient became blind.
    The case was brought before the Qadi (a Muslim judge), who ruled that no compensation was recoverable, for if the patient had not been a jackass, he would have not sought treatment with a vet!

Consumers Are Influenced by Personal and Social Factors

Choosing Wine (France)

A customer entered a grocery store and asked for a bottle of wine.
"White or red?" asked the grocer.
"It doesn't matter," answered the man. "I'm blind."

Francine and Marcel (France)

"Darling," said Francine to her husband Marcel, "You know, the other day I saw a dream of a dress for one hundred seventy francs. PLEASE let me buy it! If I don't hurry up, one of my friends is going to have it. That thought alone makes me sick ..."

Marcel was indifferent. For eight whole days he refused to yield. Then, tired of the bickering and dickering, he gave in.

"Here you are, Francine. Take these two hundred francs and go buy yourself that dress..."

Overcome with joy, Francine left the house and headed to the store. An hour later she returned.

"Well dear," asked Marcel, "what about that dress?"

"Mon cheri, the dress is still in the store. It did not interest anyone for eight days, so why should I buy it?"

The Dominant Feature

"I've come back to buy the car you showed me yesterday," said the customer as he stepped into the auto showroom.

"That's fine," the salesman said. "I thought you'd be back. Now, tell me what was the dominant feature that made you decide to buy this car?"

"My wife," replied the man.

Smart Consumers
Search for Information

A Qualified Pharmacist (Spain)

A customer entered a pharmacy.
"Are you the pharmacist?"
"Yes, sir."
"For how long have you been practicing this profession?"
"For thirty years, sir."
"And where is your diploma?"
"It's hanging right in front of you, sir."
"Well then, give me one aspirin."

Marketers Work Hard
to Satisfy Customers

Frogs' Legs (France)

"Waiter, do you have frogs' legs?"
"Oh no, monsieur! It's my rheumatism that makes me walk like this!"

Full Service

A man entered a restaurant and tied the white napkin around his neck. The owner asked one of his waiters to tell the patron that what he did was not practiced in his restaurant. The waiter did not want to insult the guest. He thought for a moment and then approached the man.
"Hello sir," said the waiter. "Would you like a haircut or a shave?"

Know Your Customer ... (France)

"Good morning, Monsieur Lenoir," said the grocer, smiling.
"Listen, my friend," said the customer, who looked pretty irritated, "you have been calling me Monsieur Lenoir for three months now. My name is Maillochart. MAIL-LO-CHART!"
"Oh, excuse me Monsieur, I'm confused, Monsieur. I'm really sorry."
"Don't mention it, my friend. No problem."
        The following morning, the same customer returned to the grocery store.
"Good morning, Monsieur Lenoir," said the grocer. "I have an interesting story for you. Yesterday morning a fellow came to my store and said his name was Polochart or maybe Maillochon, I can't recall exactly. Anyhow, he looked so much like you, almost like a twin brother!"

Wrong Reason

At a flower shop:
"Mr. Cohen, how about buying a nice bouquet of flowers for the woman you love?"
"Impossible. I'm a married man."

Consumer's Taste

Joe: "Waiter, is this prune or apple strudel?"
Waiter: "Can't you tell from the taste?"
Joe: "No, I can't."
Waiter: "Well, then what difference does it make?"

Personal Service (Israel)

A meshugener (Yiddish: crazy person) went to see the hospital director, whom he found sitting in his office, petting his dog.
"I'd like to speak to you," said the meshugener.
"Go ahead!" said the director.
Pointing at the dog, the meshugener said: "I would like to speak to you alone if possible!"

Adapting to Customer's Needs (Arabic fable)

Once Juha was working in the house of a very rich man. He was carrying water, bringing woods, cooking food, preparing coffee, shopping for groceries, in short - he was doing everything he was told to do. One day the landlord told him:

"I'd like to eat something good. What's your opinion about eggplants?"

"There is nothing better than the eggplant," said Juha. "You can eat it as salad, as patties, fried, cooked, anyway you like it. It's very tasty and good for your health and also for your nerves."

"Really?" asked the landlord.

"Sure!" answered Juha.

"And why don't I feel well when I eat eggplants?" asked the landlord, "why do I feel sick every time I eat? I think it's not such a healthy vegetable."

"True," said Juha, "it's bitter and it's black and it's not so good for a man's health."

"Really?" asked the landlord.

"Yeah," replied Juha.

"How come you're now saying the opposite of what you said before?"

"Look, Sir," said Juha. "I'm working for you - not for the eggplants!"

A Fussy Customer

She was one of those fussy women who sometimes come into restaurants.

"I want my egg fried exactly 2 minutes. The white part should be done real nice, but I don't want the yolk to get too hard. About half a pinch of salt ... no more, no less. A sniff of pepper. Oh, yes, make sure the frying pan isn't too greasy. And I like my eggs straight from the country."

"One thing, lady," said the waitress ever so sweetly, the hen's name is Doris. Is that all right?"

6. Segmenting and Targeting Consumers

Marketers recognize that different consumers have different needs. They design products and services to accommodate people with different tastes and budgets.

Illustrating Market Segmentation

Travelling Third Class (Bulgaria)

A well-dressed, rich Gabrovonian travelled third class on the train. It was a very hot summer day and the train was terribly crowded.

"Sir," a gypsy said to him, "why should you, of all people, travel third class?"

"Because there is no fourth," replied the Gabrovonian.

Buying Presents

A man was looking at some neckties and tossed one or two aside contemptuously. Noticing that the clerk put those he had so vehemently rejected into a separate box, he asked:

"What becomes of those?"

"We sell them to women who want to buy presents for men."

No Discrimination

"Do you serve chicken here?"

"Certainly, we cater to everyone!"

Finding Good Customers is Tough

A Loyal Customer

A San Francisco bank cashier cashed six phony checks for the same forger within a two-week period. When police and the bank's manager asked the girl why she suspected nothing and kept cashing the checks, she explained: "Because he looked familiar!"

Nasrudin the Shrewd Shopper (Turkey)

Nasrudin went into a shop. First, he picked up a pair of trousers but then changed his mind and asked to replace them with a shirt that had an identical price. When he was ready to leave, the merchant shouted:
"You have not paid!"
"But I left you the trousers, which were of the same value as the shirt."
"But you did not pay for the trousers either!"
"Of course not," said the Mulla, "why should I pay for something I did not buy?"

Why Fight?

A tall Irish fellow entered a local bar.
"Give me a double whisky before the fight starts!"
Two minutes later he ordered:
"Another double whisky, before the fight starts!"
    While he was sipping his drink, the barman asked him:
"Tell me, friend, why do you think there is going to be a fight here?"
"Because I don't have any money to pay for my drinks!"

She Went to the Market (Russia)

A salesperson knocked at the door. A little girl opened.
"Hi, may I see your father?"
"He is not at home," replied the girl, "but he'll return in eight hours, forty minutes and twenty three seconds. He is traveling around the globe in a space shuttle right now."
"Then may I see your mother?"
"She is not at home either," said the girl.
"When will she be back?"
"One can never know. She went to the market!"

Serving Customers Both Ways

A store manager interviewed a potential sales clerk.
"Do you know how to serve customers?" she asked.
"Yes ma'am, both ways!" replied the man.
"And what do you mean by 'both ways'"?
"One way so they will come back and the other so they won't!"

Self-Defense

The man in the barber chair signalled with his finger:
"Got another razor?" he whispered.
"Why?" asked the barber.
"I'd like to defend myself!" replied the customer.

Tipping (Bulgaria)

Two Gabrovonians had a bet as to which one would leave less tip in a restaurant.
After the meal, one of them dropped one stotinka (equivalent to one penny) on the table and looked triumphantly at the other.
"That was for both of us," the second said humbly to the waiter who came to collect the bill.

Savings (Bulgaria)

A Gabrovonian got off the train and asked a taxi driver:
"How much do you charge for a ride to the city center?"
"Two leva. Jump in!"
"No, thanks. I was asking to find out how much I'm saving."

A Conscientious Customer (Russia)

Hershele was window-shopping in the market. An old lady with a runny nose tried to solicit him to enter her store.
"Sir, have a look, we carry all kinds of merchandise!"
"And handkerchiefs," asked Hershele, "do you carry handkerchiefs?"
"Handkerchiefs you said? Hundreds of them!" boasted the lady; "cotton, rayon, silk handkerchiefs!"
"Well then, take one and wipe your nose," advised Hershele.

Who Should Owe What?

Joseph wanted to open a grocery store. He went to a local bank and asked for $10,000. After a few months with no response, he wrote the bank a reminder, saying: "you owe me an answer."

A week later he received a note from the bank: "Better we should owe you an answer than you should owe us $10,000."

Only Ten (France)

Mrs. Roland got a can of green peas at the local grocery store.

"You know," said the grocer, "I wish I had ten customers like you!"

"Well," said the woman, surprised, "I owe you 756 Francs and you would like to have ten customers like me?"

"Yes," said the grocer, "because customers like you I happen to have at least fifty..."

A Caring Customer

Khaimovich ran out to the pharmacy at 3:00 AM and frantically knocked at the door. After a while, the pharmacist came out in his pajamas and robe.
"What do you want at this hour?" asked the sleepy shop owner.
"Do you by any chance have any ink for sale?" inquired Khaimovich.
"No, we don't!" said the annoyed pharmacist.
Khaimovich returned home, searched his apartment, and returned to the pharmacy a few minutes later.
"What do you want NOW?" shouted the pharmacist.
"Well, I just found a bottle of ink at home and came by to bring you some," responded Khaimovich.

Voice of the Customer

At a restaurant during the breakfast hour a man asked a waitress for the lone piece of dried-up French toast left in the warming tray. She refused to give it to him, telling him that a fresh batch would be along in a minute. He replied that he would take it anyhow. The waitress, adamant, insisted that he wait for a fresh piece.
"Look lady," he shouted, "If I wanted to fight for breakfast I would have stayed home!"

Checking IDs (Turkey)

Nasrudin went into a bank with a check to cash.
"Can you identify yourself?" asked the teller.
Nasrudin took out a mirror and looked into it.
"Yep, that's me!" he said.

Two Croissants (France)

A man entered a coffee shop and said:
"I'd like cafe au lait and two croissants."
"I'm sorry, sir," said the waiter, "I'm already out of croissants."
"Okay," said the fellow, "then bring me a demi and two croissants."
"Sir, you didn't understand me. I told you I don't have any more croissants."
"Oh well, then, let it be a cup of tea and two croissants."
"But sir, I've already told you twice, I have no croissants left!"
   At this point another customer intervened:
"I say, you're extremely patient, waiter. In your place I'd have shoved those two croissants in his mouth long ago..."

Pleasing Customers Is an Art

No Complaints

For his first six years the child did not say a word. His parents were led to believe that their son was mute.
One evening at the dinner table the child opened his mouth and said: "The food is too salty."
   Now the parents were speechless. After a few minutes, the father asked: "How come you haven't talked for six years?"
"Up until now," said the child, "I've had no complaints!"

The Customer Is Always Right (Poland)

Isaac and Pinkhas, two merchants, had a business dispute and came to the rabbi's house to settle it. As usual, the rebbetsen (the rabbi's wife) was also at home.

The rabbi listened to Isaac patiently, and then said:
"Isaac, you're right!"

Then Pinkhas voiced his complaint. When he finished, the rabbi ruled:
"Pinkhas, you are right!"

The rebbetsen, who could not control herself any longer, interrupted and argued:
"May you be healthy and strong, Rabbi! How is it possible that both of them are right? When one wins, the other one must lose!"

The rabbi thought for a moment and then replied:
"you are also right!"

The Customer Is Always Right (France)

The manager of the mens' shoe department heard a loud argument in the store. Approaching the noisy area, he said to the sales clerk:
"How come you were arguing with the person who just left the store? Don't you know that here the customer is always right?"
"This is exactly what our discussion was about," explained the young sales clerk. "He insisted vehemently that he was wrong!"

Empathy for the Customer

Doctor to patient: "Your heart functions wonderfully, a
your lungs are entirely normal. Only your legs are still
swollen. But that does not bother me."
Patient to Doctor: "Believe me Doctor, if your legs were
swollen, it wouldn't bother me either."

Selling Effectiveness

Working in a candy store, Martha always had customers
lined up waiting for her service while all the other
salesladies were standing there, twiddling their thumbs.
The store manager noted her popularity and asked her for
her secret.
"It's easy enough," Martha replied. "The other girls scoop
up more than a pound of candy and then start taking away.
I always scoop up less than a pound and then add to it."

Getting Good Service

A company executive uses the same routine every time he
checks into a hotel. He casually tells the operator to get
the White House on the phone. Then he asks to speak to
the President. His second call is to the Vice-President.
"I never get them on the phone," he told his friends, "but
from then on, I'm always sure to receive great service at
the hotel."

A Full-Service Restaurant

A brash man entered a high-priced restaurant, selected a choice table, sat down and unfolded a napkin in his lap. He poured a glass of water from the carafe and then unwrapped a package of home-made sandwiches.

When the astonished manager came over to protest, the sandwich-eater demanded:

"Who are you?"

"I am the manager!" came the icy reply.

"Just the man I want to see. Why isn't the orchestra playing?"

7. Developing Marketing Strategies

Information obtained through situation analysis is used to develop a marketing strategy. This involves selecting target consumers, and aligning the product, place, price and promotion to serve them profitably.

Illustrating Marketing Strategies

A Good Strategy (Turkey)

Mulla Nasrudin used to stand on the street corner on market-days, and no matter how often people offered him a choice between a large and a small coin, he always chose the smaller one. One day a kind man advised him:
"Mulla, you should take the bigger coin. Then you will have more money."
"That might be true," said Nasrudin, "but if I always take the bigger one - people will stop offering me money!"

An Ailing Strategy (Russia)

The president of a clothing company discussed the following problem with one his sales managers:
"I have a huge overstock of blouses. They cost us four rubles each. What can I do to get rid of them?"
"Here is a good strategy," said the manager, "we'll ship five blouses to each of our customers and attach a note saying that we're delighted to send our preferred customers four of our best blouses for four rubles a piece.
When they find five blouses instead of four in the package, they'll get tickled to death, and we'll get rid of the blouses."
"I like your idea!" said the president.
A few weeks later, each one of the customers sent back four blouses and attached a note saying: "These blouses are not fashionable any more."

ier Pearce bought Farmer Perkins' cow for $100 cash.

kins got to thinking that since Pearce paid the price so willingly, the cow must be worth more. The next day he bought the cow back for $200. Later, Pearce used the same reasoning and bought the cow back - for $300. This kept going on until the price went up to $1,500.

A cowboy from another town heard about the valuable cow and rode his horse to Perkins' farm. He bought the cow from Perkins for $2,000. When Pearce found out about it he hurried over to Perkins and reprimanded him:

"You are a fool, selling this cow. Both of us were making such a good living off of her!"

Good Strategists Have Bold Vision

Bold Vision (China)

Two men were short-sighted but instead of admitting it boasted of sharp vision.

One day they heard that a tablet was to be hung in a temple. Each one found out what was written on it beforehand. When the day came, they both went to the temple. Looking up, one said:

"Look, aren't the characters 'Brightness and Unbrightness'"?

"And the smaller ones -- There! You can't see them! They say, 'Written by so and so in a certain month, on a certain day!'" said the other.

A passer-by asked what they were looking at. When told, the man laughed.

"The tablet hasn't been hoisted up, so how can you see the characters?" he asked.

Controlling Costs Helps
Increase Profits

Business Interruptions (Poland)

A busy merchant came to the rabbi, complaining:
"Rabbi, lots of people come to my store just to chat and my business is interrupted. What should I do?"
After giving some thought to the problem, the rabbi replied:
"This is my advice to you, son. If a rich man comes to you, ask him for charity, and he'll not come back. If a poor man comes, you lend him some money, and rest assured you are not going to see his face any more!"

Minimizing Loss (Spain)

"I can't understand how you run your business," said the Marketing Consultant to the shopkeeper. "When you sell on credit you also offer a discount?"
"Well," replied the shopkeeper, "it is well known that people do not pay their debts. By giving them a discount, I lose less money!"

8. Product Management

Product Management involves decisions related to the goods and services a company offers. The jokes in this section can be told in relation to one of the following topics:

1. What products, features, and services to offer
2. How to determine product quality
3. What services should come with the product
4. How to obtain brand recognition
5. How to package the product
6. how many sizes to offer

Marketers Offer Products
to Different Market Segments

Two Ham Sandwiches (Belgium)

This dialogue was heard around a Belgian fast-food
counter.
"Two ham sandwiches please, one of them without
mustard."
"Which one of them do you want without mustard?"

Mr. Thomas had three swimming pools built in the back yard of his new mansion. One day he invited one of his friends over, and proudly showed him the house.

"Why do you need so many swimming pools?" his friend asked.

"One has cold water, the other one hot water and the third is empty," replied Thomas.

"Cold water I can understand," said the friend. "I can also understand hot water. But empty, without any water? what for?"

"You have no idea," said the rich man, "how many friends I have, who do not know to swim!"

Kinds of Salt (Germany)

Kurt entered a grocery store and asked for five cents worth of salt.

"What kind of salt?" asked the grocer, Mr. Hoffman.

"How many kinds of salt are there?"

"Come with me to my cellar!"

In the cellar Hoffman showed Kurt no less than 40 or 50 barrels of salt. Kurt was amazed.

"All these are different salts?" he asked.

"Yes. They are different. We have salt for all kinds of prices and uses."

"My goodness, you are a specialist. I suppose if you have all these barrels of different kinds of salt, you must sell lots of it!"

"Oh," said Hoffman, "me, I'm not so good at selling salt, but the guy who sold it to me -- boy, can he sell salt..."

Color TV (Egypt)

"Do you carry color-TVs?"
"Yes, Sir."
"I'd like a red one, please!"

Shape Matters (France)

Pierre walked into a bakery.

"I'd like to order a cake in the shape of the letter S," he said. "Can you do that?"

"Sure," said the baker,"we can make a cake in any shape. When would you like it to be ready?"

"Have it ready by three o'clock tomorrow."

The next day Pierre showed up at the bakery. The cake was ready for him, shaped like an S and decorated beautifully.

"Oh," said Pierre, "that's not what I wanted. You made it in the shape of a regular printed S. I wanted a graceful script S!"

"I'm terribly sorry, sir. I'll make you another cake at no extra charge. Come back at six o'clock."

At six o'clock Pierre came back, looked at the cake and said:

"That's perfect. Just what I wanted."

"I'm delighted, sir," said the baker. "Now tell me, what kind of a box should I put it in?"

"Oh, don't bother wrapping it, sir," said Pierre, "I'll eat it here!"

Product Development
Requires Creativity

Raising Chicken (Russia)

The Russian minister of agriculture was touring some farms. He came upon a farm managed by a fellow named

Ivanov.

"What do you feed your chicken with?" asked the minister.

"We buy seeds for them, Sir."

"What?! when there is such a shortage of wheat all over the country?" thundered the minister, "you're fired!"

The minister continued his tour and arrived to a farm managed by the Ukraine Galushko.

"What do you feed your chicken with?" asked the minister.

"We give them corn," was Galushko's answer.

The minister thundered, furious as hell:

"We are importing corn from Canada and pay with gold! You're arrested!"

The next stop was in Rabinovich's farm.

"What do you feed your chicken with, Mr. Rabinovich?"

"Comrade minister," answered Rabinovich, "we give each chicken a ruble and tell them to buy their food on their own!"

Product Design

An architect was having a difficult time with a prospective home builder.

"Can't you at least give me an idea of the type of house you want to build?" pleaded the architect.

The man hesitated, then replied:

"Well, all I can tell you is it must go with an antique doorknob my wife bought in Boston."

71

That's What Chairs Are For

A lady went into an antique furniture store and said:
"Last week I bought here half a dozen chairs and three of
them are already broken!"
"Impossible!" replied the old man. "Perhaps someone was
sitting on them?"

New Product

"I think your husband is wearing a new kind of suit," said Rose.

"Not at all," said Lily.

"Well, he looks different," persisted Rose.

"It's a new husband," explained Lily.

"Tan"

A young lady, beautifully tanned, entered a swimming suit store. She tried on lots of suits and did not like any of them. Finally she said to the exhausted sales clerk:

"What I really am looking for is a swimming suit that will enable me to complete my tan in all the white places."

Improved Service Helps Obtain a Competitive Advantage

How Do You Take Your Coffee?

Mike went into a diner.

"I'd like a cup of coffee without cream," he requested.

The waitress came back in a few minutes and said: "I'm sorry, sir, but we're already out of cream. Would you mind taking your coffee without milk?"

Shorter Waiting Lines (Russia)

A sign on a government agency's door read:
"From now on this office will be open from 8:00 to 12:00 instead of 7:00 to 12:00, as it was until now. This way the lines will be one hour shorter everyday, for the benefit of the public."

Full Service

A small town drugstore went out of business. The ex-owner posted this notice on his window:
"These services, formerly available here, can be obtained as follows:

      Ice water at fountain in park.
      General information from cop at the corner.
      Change for a dollar at bank.
      Matches and scratch paper at hotel.
      Rest rooms at home.
      Magazine for browsing at doctor's office.
      Bus information at the terminal.
      And -
      Loafing at any other location of your own choosing."

Some Marketers Try Hard to Provide Good Quality

Hearing Aids (Poland)

Two old ladies bought new hearing aids from the town doctor. One bright sunny morning one of them met the other on the corner of the street.
"Good morning, Freina!"
"Good morning, Sheina!" said Freina, who was already loaded with produce bought at the market.
Asked Sheina:
"What time do you have?"
Answered Freina:
"I carry radishes!"

A Small Steak

A guy entered a restaurant. He ordered a steak and got a small piece, tough as a shoe sole. He called the waiter:
"Was it worth it to kill a whole cow for such a small piece?"
"First," replied the waiter, "it was not a cow. Second, we did not kill it. It died on its own."

Being at the Right Place at the Right Time

A tourist entered the hotel manager's office, complaining:
"This morning at ten, when I was going to take a shower, the bathroom was full of flies!"
"Well, next time take your shower during lunch time," advised the manager. "At this time all the flies flock to the dining room!"

A Wedding Suit (Poland)

Abe Kaplan took his son to Mendel the tailor.
"My son is going to get married, Mendel. I would like him to have a very beautiful suit. A suit that nobody will laugh at."
"Relax, Mr. Kaplan," said Mendel, "you don't have to worry. I've not heard anybody laughing at my work. I've only heard them crying about it!"

Good Luck (Poland)

A guy entered a tobacco store and bought a cigar. A few minutes later he showed up in the store again, this time extremely angry.

"I've asked for the best cigar, and you've given me the most stinking one, the worst I've ever had!"

"You're really lucky," was the owner's reaction, "you have one cigar and I have a whole store full of them!"

Just Sign It Yourself

Here is a letter transcribed exactly as a daydreaming secretary took it down.

"Dear Mr. Umpstead:

Let's see. What'll I tell the old jackass. In reply to yours of the sixteenth we are surprised to learn the super-power two-ton used truck you purchased from us is not giving perfect satisfaction. We had to sell it quick before it fell to pieces.

As you know, Mr. Umpstead, we inspect all used cars thoroughly before turning them over to the purchaser. Your truck was in excellent condition when it left our garage. That's a swell dress you have on. New, isn't it?

It is possible your driver is at fault. Four miles to the gallon is very poor mileage for a truck in such good condition as yours. Four gallons to a mile would be about right. I never noticed before you had a dimple in your chin. Bring it around and we will have our expert mechanic make the proper adjustments.

Sincerely yours,

Just sign it yourself."

Hotel Services

A guest was just about to write his name on the register of a hotel in a small midwest town when he saw a bed bug crawling across the page.

"Well, this is the limit," he said. "I've been bitten by fleas in Missouri, mosquitoes in Jersey, horseflies in Maine, and chiggers in Kansas - but this is the first place I've ever been in where a bug looked over the hotel register to see the number of my room!"

First Come, First Served (Russia)

Two fathers-to-be were pacing impatiently in the corridor in front of the delivery room at one of Moscow's hospitals. After some time, a nurse came out and approached one of them:

"Congratulations, comrade, you have a baby boy!"

"This is unheard of!" shouted the other guy, "I was here long before this man, so how come you take care of him first? What kind of a service do you offer here?"

Service and Quality (Poland)

A very angry man entered a watch repair shop, yelling at the owner:

"You good-for-nothing, you! Until you repaired my watch, at least sometimes it was working. Now it doesn't work at all. Never. Just stopped. That's all. You ruined it!"

"How could I ruin it? All the time it was here I never touched it!"

Aroma in a Roman Restaurant (Italy)

Mario entered a small restaurant in Rome with his wife. Mario ordered fish and his wife ordered veal.

Mario was about to taste his food when he stopped, fork in mid-air, and sniffed suspiciously. He sniffed again, this time wrinkling his nose in disgust, and then called the waiter.

"This fish positively stinks!" he said.

"I'm afraid you're mistaken, mister," countered the waiter.

"But smell it yourself. I tell you, it stinks!"

"And I tell you, sir, you are mistaken. It isn't your fish; it's your wife's veal cutlet that stinks!"

Price and Quality

A Russian woman went to a bakery.

"How much is this one?" she asked, pointing to a loaf of bread.

"Nine rubles," said the baker.

"Nine rubles for the bread? You're crazy! Seven rubles, that's enough."

"Look, lady. For seven rubles I would have to make the bread worse. And as God is my witness, I couldn't make the bread any worse than it already is!"

Jet Service (England)

It was reported one day that a Concorde had left Heathrow with one passenger. A spokesman, asked about this somewhat curious state of affairs, replied:
"We never expected the service to be overcrowded."

Marketers Help Consumers Understand Quality

How to Grow a Mustache

"Can you prove that this hair tonic is effective?" a bald-headed customer asked his druggist.
"Of course," answered the druggist, "one lady customer of mine pulled the cork off of the bottle using her teeth and twenty-four hours later she had a mustache!"

Product Durability

Sales clerk: "This pair of shoes will last you forever."
Customer: "All right, I'll take it."
Sales clerk: "Here they are, sir, and please come back when you need similar shoes again!"

Many Sellers Offer
Product Warranties

Full Satisfaction or Your Money Back

Pat brought an empty cough medicine bottle back to the pharmacist.
"You told me that if it was not satisfactory I'd get my money back."

The pharmacist counted out the money and placed it on the counter beside the bottle.

Pat pushed the money back toward the clerk:
"Now, give me another bottle."

Customers Use Products Differently

Product Benefits (Russia)

Two Russians are sitting and rolling cigarettes in the factory's cafeteria.
"Hey, comrade," asked one of them, "what do you think about 'Pravda'"?
"The truth? I've never tried smoking it."

Some Sellers Offer Financing

Buying with Credit (France)

The following conversation took place at a car dealership:
Customer: "If I buy one of these cars on credit, how long will I have to pay for it?"
Salesperson: "It depends on how much you can pay each month."
Customer: "Hmm... fifteen francs, more or less."
Salesperson (laughing): "Well then, it will take you about a hundred years."
Customer: "Good. As far as I'm concerned, it fits me perfectly!..."

Marketers Try
to Differentiate Products

Two Horses

Farmer Joe bought two horses. To tell them apart, he immediately cut off the tail of one. The next day, the second horse got his tail caught in a machine and half of the tail was gone. Then Joe knocked out a tooth in the first one, again wishing to be able to tell the two apart. An hour later, the second horse ran into the barn door and lost a tooth. The farmer discussed the problem with one of his helpers, who suggested that maybe the horses were not exactly of the same height. So Joe got the horses and had them stand side by side:
"You're a genius," he told his helper. "The white horse is taller than the black one! Now I can tell them apart!"

Mr. Klein

A rancher called the legal firm of Klein, Klein, Klein and Klein. The conversation went as follows:
"Hello, I'd like to talk to Mr. Klein."
"Mr. Klein is in court."
"Oh, then I'll talk to Mr. Klein."
"He's in conference."
"Well, then I'll talk to Mr. Klein."
"Mr. Klein isn't in today. He's playing golf."
"Oh, in that case, may I talk to Mr. Klein?"
"Speaking."

A Brand Name Should Be
Short and Easy to Remember

Kremenchutzky, Kamenetzky, and Levin (Russia)

Two friends opened a clothing store and named it after themselves: "Kremenchutzky and Kamenetzky."

Business never picked up because customers could not pronounce the store's name. As a result, Kremenchutzky volunteered to change his last name to Levin. The sign outside the store was changed to read - "Levin and Kamenetzky."

More customers started to show up, but they all asked for Levin. Kamenetzky felt neglected, so he decided to change his name to Levin too. Again, the sign was changed. This time it read: "Levin and Levin."

The next day, the first customer entered. "Good morning, is Mr. Levin in today?"

"Which one," came the quick response, "Kremenchutzky or Kamenetzky?"

A Good Brand Name
is Crucial for Success

What's in a Name?

Three Jewish immigrants, Goldsmith, Silverstein and Schneider arrived in New York soon after the end of the

First World War. Soon after, each went his way.

Ten years later they had a reunion in New York. All three looked prosperous, and couldn't wait to tell their success stories. Goldsmith began.

"You know, I did not know what to do, so I went into the gold business because of my name. I was just plain lucky! I became a rich man."

Then Silverstein recounted:

"The same thing happened to me - because of my name I went into the silver business, and it was a lucky break for me. Thank God, I do very well!"

Schneider smiled.

"You know, my name means 'tailor' so I decided to become a tailor. It's an honest living. I opened my own store and called it 'Taylor's,' spelling it with a Y, to be a little fancy. But business was terrible. Just awful. I didn't know how to bring in customers.

One day, when I was praying in the synagogue, I made a 'neder' (a solemn vow) that if God helped me in my business, I'd give half my profits to Him. And then like a miracle, business picked up. I hired more people, I opened new shops, and expanded into retailing. Now, thank God, I do very well. Maybe you've heard of my chain of stores? I call it 'Lord and Taylor's.'"

Take It for Nothing

"Gimme a dime's worth of asafetida. Dad wants you to charge it."
"All right; what's your name?"
"Shermerhorn."
"Take it for nothing ... I ain't going to spell asafetida and Shermerhorn for no dime!"

Trademark (France)

A woman entered a specialty store and asked if they could sell her artificial breasts.

"Certainly, Madame," said the lady at the counter.

"What brand are they?" asked the woman.

"I don't know," answered the sales clerk, "but don't worry. This store carries only registered trademarks. We don't carry imitations!"

Value of a Name (Egypt)

Ibn Samir, a neighbor of Abu Doulaf the famous poet of Baghdad, accumulated a lot of debts. To pay his creditors he decided to sell his house and asked one thousand dinars for it. "But your house is not worth more than five hundred dinars!" everyone commented. "How can you expect to sell it for one thousand?"

"I'm selling the house for only five hundred dinars, and the neighborhood of Abu Doulaf for another five hundred dinars," replied Ibn Samir.

When Abu Doulaf heard about this remark he was so moved that he paid off all Ibn Samir's debts and told him:

"I don't wish to lose you as my neighbor!"

Buying a Saddle

If one man calls you a horse, pay no attention. If a second man calls you a horse, think it over. If a third man calls you a horse, buy a saddle!

The Right Product Leads to Customer Satisfaction

Milk and Cognac (Spain)

A farmer was going every week to the hospital to visit his sick old mother. Every visit he brought her a bottle of milk, into which, unbeknownst to her, he had poured a good amount of cognac. Each time she finished drinking the milk without commenting. One day, however, she whispered to her son:

"Listen, Pedro, can I ask you a favor?"

"Anything you want, mom," he replied.

"I beg you dear, no matter what happens, never sell this cow!"

Sellers Must Carry the Right Sizes

The Right Size

Harry bought material for a suit and brought it to Schneider, the tailor.

"Mr. Schneider," he asked, "is this enough material?"

"No," replied Schneider. "It will never do."

So Harry went to the tailor shop across the street that belonged to Hirsch. Hirsch measured the material carefully and said:

"Yes, there's enough."

When Harry came to pick up his suit he was amazed to see that Hirsch's little boy was wearing a suit made out of the same material as his own.

"See here," he said to Hirsch, "Schneider said there wasn't enough material, and yet you made me a suit out of it, and had enough left over to make a suit for your boy?"

"Well," replied Hirsch, "for my little boy the material was just enough. But Schneider has a son twice as big as mine!"

Fitting the Right Size

"Do you carry pillow cases?"
"Yes, Sir. What size do you need?"
"I really don't know, but I wear a size seven hat."

Convenient Packaging Adds Value

Value Packaging

Zelda entered a store in the Bronx and asked the shopkeeper:
"What is the price of a herring?"
"Six cents a piece," answered Katz, the shopkeeper.
In the meantime, Zelda overheard the owner of the next store announcing his merchandise:
"Ladies, cheap! Five cents a herring!"
"Do you hear that?" Zelda asked, "why do you charge more?"
"Because," answered Katz, "I wrap the herring in today's newspaper and my neighbor uses week-old ones!"

Package Value (Arabic fable)

One day Karakash the Justice of Peace met Abu-Nawas in the public bath. They were sitting on an Italian marble bench, talking and philosophizing about everything.

"The times now are changing," said the judge. "Everything costs so much money. The worst house-worker will not work for less than one majida (an old Turkish coin) a month. And give him food and give him clothing. Give him this and give him that and still he is not happy."

"True, that's how it is," agreed Abu-Nawas.

"Once, you would go to the marketplace, buy a young and strong slave and he would work for you for food and clothing only. These were the good times!"

Abu-Nawas nodded with approval and did not say anything. A few minutes later, said Karakash the judge: "The public bath, what does it do to people?"

"What does it do to people? It makes people clean!" said Abu-Nawas.

"That's right," said Karakash. "But there is much more to it. I think the bath makes all people equal, more or less. Without clothes, all are equal. Rich man, poor man, merchant, government worker, porter, judge - everyone looks the same. Why? because they don't wear their clothes. Take me, for instance. Without the court clothes I look like a regular man -- like you. Worthless. If you came to buy me as a slave today, how much would you give for me?"

Abu-Nawas thought for a few seconds, then said: "I would not give more than five dinar."

"What do you mean five dinar? only the towel I have on me is worth five dinar!"

"That's true," said Abu-Nawas. "I have already taken that into account!"

Sellers Decide How Much Product to Put in a Package

Doubling Sales

Ed had just finished drinking his second glass of beer at the bar. He turned to the manager and said:
"How many kegs of beer do you sell here in a week?"
"Thirty five," the manager answered with pride.
"Well, I've just thought of a way you can sell seventy."
        The manager was startled.
"How?" he asked.
"Simple. Fill up the glasses!"

Two Birds

Babcock entered a pet store and saw a canary that could sing several songs.

"How much?" asked Babcock.

"Two hundred dollars," said the proprietor, "and you have to buy this other bird with him."

"Two hundred is steep enough," sighed Babcock. "Why do I have to buy this other bird as well?"

"The canary needs him," said the proprietor. "That's his arranger!"

How Many Donkeys? (Arabic fable)

When he grew up, Juha went to work as a donkey driver. The workers were loading sacks of sand on his ten donkeys and Juha used to take them to the site where a new building was being built.

Sunday, before he hit the road, he counted the donkeys to be sure no one was missing. He saw he had exactly ten, and started to walk. He reached the new-building place, unloaded the sand, mounted his donkey, and returned.

Once on the road, he counted the donkeys and saw he had only nine. He got off his donkey, lined up all of them, counted again and realized no one was missing. He mounted his donkey again and continued. While the donkeys were walking, he began thinking, how come he counted only nine before, and ten later. And then he thought, maybe he had a mistake. Maybe he did not count right. He counted the donkeys again, and again there were only nine. He got off his donkey, lined all of them up again, counted them very slowly, using his fingers to help him -- everything was okay. There were ten. He was really amazed and could not understand why one time he had nine and the other time he had ten donkeys. He counted once more, both ways, and again, each time got a different result.

In the meantime, the builder noticed it was taking him very long to deliver the sand, and decided to go look for Juha. He found Juha on the road, counting the donkeys. The builder listened to Juha's story, and then said:

"Juha, get off your donkey, stand in the end of the line, and I'll count this time."

He counted the donkeys using his fingers, and said: "It's really confusing. Before, there were ten; and now I see eleven donkeys!"

Convenient Packaging

At the grocery store:
"Five pounds of coffee, please."
"Yes, anything else today?"
"No, thanks. And if it isn't too heavy a package, I'll take it with me."
"Oh no, Sir, it'll only weigh three or four pounds."

9. Place (Distribution)

"Place" is the name used for "distribution channels."
Distribution channels include suppliers, producers,
wholesalers, retailers and agents who help consumers
obtain product at the right place and at the right time. In
this section you will find jokes that relate to the following
topics:
1.   Should direct or indirect distribution be used
2.   What services should retailers provide
3.   How can consumers be reached at the right time and
      place

An Indirect Distribution
Includes Middlemen

The Middleman (Arabic fable)

When two do not agree on something, they will be better off settling their disagreement with nobody in between, because the one who stands in the middle in order to make peace, always wants to gain something. He does not care if both sides lose. It is always like this. The one who stays in the middle between the buyer and the seller takes from the former, and from the latter too:

Once two cats snatched a piece of cheese from the table and carried it outside. Immediately they started fighting. One said the whole piece was his, and the other said the whole piece was his. Finally one of them said:
"Let's divide it in two."
"Great," said the other, "I'll divide it."
"No, my dear," protested the first one. "I'll divide it."
And the fighting went on. Then one said:
"Why should we have a war between us, when we both are dying to eat? Let's go to a judge. He will divide the cheese into two equal pieces. And thus justice will prevail!"
"Fine," said the other. "I agree. Let's go."
And they went to the Fox and told him their story. They asked him to take the cheese and divide it equally for them.
"That's exactly what I'm doing," said Abu-Saliman the fox. He broke the cheese to two pieces, one bigger and one smaller, and laid each piece on a scale. He saw that the bigger piece went down on the scale, took a bite out of it to equate it to the other piece. But the bastard, he

purposely ate more than he needed, so that the smaller piece was now bigger... And what did he do then? He took the piece that was small before and now became big - and took a bite from it, too, exactly as he had before. He proceeded this way, eating and biting once from here and once from there without any discrimination at all.

"Stop it! Enough!" shouted the two cats when they saw he was about to finish it altogether. "Leave the cheese alone and we will divide it ourselves!"

"For you it's maybe enough," replied the fox, "but not for me. You wanted exactly two halves? You wanted justice? You'll have justice! For the sake of justice I'm ready to work as much as it takes, until the cheese will be in exactly two equal halves!"

And Abu-Saliman the fox continued eating from here and from there till he finished all the cheese and the cats remained as hungry as they were before and maybe even more.

Cutting the Middleman (Poland)

Ruben was a very successful wholesaler who managed a huge business. He would take out a loan with the Barclis bank, and when the time came to pay it back, he would take out a loan with the National bank. Thus, he would pay Barclis bank with money borrowed from the National bank, and the National bank with money from Barclis bank. Three years he managed his finances in this fashion.

One day he got fed-up and stopped paying altogether. Pretty soon the banks were after him.

"What's the matter with you?! Do I have to run from Barclis to National bank and from National to Barclis? Why can't you pay each other directly? I'm not going to be your middleman anymore. Enough is enough!"

Efficient Distributors Are Accessible

The Doctor and the Plumber

The doctor called his plumber at 2:00 a.m. with an emergency leak in the bathroom.

"Tell you what," the plumber said half asleep. "Take two aspirins, drop them down the pipe, and call me in the morning if the leak hasn't cleared up by then!"

Some Products are Distributed by Mail

An Order Slip

A Wyoming cowboy wrote to a mail-order house asking for toilet paper. He received a note directing him to use the order slip on page 998 of their catalogue.
"If I had your catalogue," the cowboy wrote back, "would I need toilet paper?"

An Order - and an Acknowledgement

"Send radio : if good, will send check."
"Send check : if good, will send radio."

Good Distributors Are Hard to Find

Channel Power

"How did you make your fortune?"
"I became an exclusive distributor of a successful manufacturer; he had the money and I had the experience."
"How did that help?"
"Now he has the experience and I have the money."

Buyer Beware

A boy visited the state's fair with his father. During their tour they came across cattle dealers who were busy buying cows, and while bargaining they were touching and caressing their cows. This aroused the child's curiosity: "Why do they do that?" he asked his father.
"That's their way to check what they buy," answered the father.
One day the child appeared in his father's office, out of breath after running all the way.
"Daddy," he said, "come quickly home! A merchant wants to buy Mom!"

Selling a Donkey (Egypt)

Juha went to the market to sell a donkey.
At the end of the day the donkey came back with $100.

Retailers Give Credit to Consumers

Buying on Credit (Poland)

A stranger entered a grocery store, picked out some items, and asked the grocer if he could write a check.
"But," said the grocer, "I don't know you at all!"
"My," said the customer, "here I cannot write checks because people don't know me, and in my own town I cannot write checks because people do know me ..."

He Will Be Back! (France)

An owner of a shoe store saw a customer leaving the store in a hurry.
"What has this guy taken out?" asked the owner
"A pair of black shoes for forty five francs," said the sales lady.
"Did he pay?"
"Only twenty francs because he forgot and left his wallet at home."
"And you let him take the shoes?"
"I did, sir, but rest assured he'll be back. I gave him two left shoes!"

The Paying Teller

"I want to know," said the grim-faced woman, "how much money my husband drew out of the bank last week."
"I cannot give you that information, madam," answered the cashier.
"You're the paying teller, aren't you?"
"Yes, but I'm not the telling payer!"

Store Guarantee

"Can you guarantee these shoes?" asked a customer after paying for a new pair of shoes he'd just bought.
"Certainly, sir. These shoes are fully guaranteed until you leave the store!"

Efficient Distributors Provide Fresh Products

Fresh Fish

"This fish is not as fresh as the one I bought here last week."

"That's impossible, sir. It came with the same shipment!"

Fresh Milk

A nagging customer, to the milkman:

"Is this milk fresh?"

"Lady, only an hour ago it was still grass!"

Just in Time

Timmy had only two pennies in his pocket when he approached the farmer and pointed to a luscious tomato hanging from a vine.

"Give you two cents for it," the boy offered.

"That kind brings a nickel," the farmer told him.

"This one?" Timmy asked, pointing to a smaller, greener and less tempting specimen. The farmer nodded in agreement.

"Okay," said Timmy, and sealed the deal by placing his two pennies in the farmer's hand, "I'll pick it up in about a week."

Efficient Distributors Provide Fast Service

Not-In-Time Delivery

Mr. Smith, the owner of a big New York Maternity Clothing store, received the following letter:
"Dear Mr. Smith: Please cancel my order for maternity dress model 18 which you were supposed to deliver six weeks ago. My delivery turned out faster than yours."

Good Distributors Keep Enough Product in Stock

Money in Stock

An Irishman heard that the bank in which he kept his savings started to hold payments. He hurried up to his bank, and went straight to the cashier.
"I'd like to withdraw my money!" he said.
"All right, sir. How do you want it?"
"Oh, I don't want it at all if you have the money. Only if you don't have it - I demand it immediately!"

Out-Of-Stock

A merchant opened an account with a big and famous bank. He started writing bad checks right and left, and after a while the bank managed to get rid of him. So he went to another bank. And the story repeated itself. One day one of his creditors called him.
"Listen," said the creditor, "your $1000 check came back!"
"What?!" shouted the guy, "how come?! Doesn't the other bank have money in stock either?!"

Selling Vodka

A Russian citizen entered a liquor store in Moscow and asked for a bottle of vodka. Said the owner:
"The price is ten rubles."
Asked the citizen:
"Why so expensive?"
"Five rubles for the vodka and five for the Democratic party," replied the owner.
Unwillingly the customer took a ten ruble bill out of his pocket, and paid. The owner of the store gave him five rubles change.
"And what is this?" asked the amazed customer
"No vodka today," came the reply.

Efficient Distributors Know
Where to Find Customers

Seeking Customers (Israel)

A Russian immigrated to Israel and received governmental support to set up a barber shop. After his first day at work he called the government office and said:
"What kind of a mess are you having there in your office? You haven't sent me a single customer!"

Christmas Sales

A newly arrived Russian immigrant decided to open a clothing store in Los Angeles. He went to the mall, entered a clothing store and asked:
"Which party do you have to belong to in order to run a store like this successfully?"
"The Christmas party," came the reply, loud and clear...

Hard Sell

A man was telling about his trip to New Mexico.
"There I was," he said, "completely surrounded by Indians. Indians on my right, on my left, behind me and in front of me. It was horrible."
"My," gasped his friend, "what in the world did you do?"
"What COULD I do?" asked the man, "I bought a blanket!"

Door-To-Door Begging (Israel)

This story took place in Tel Aviv. A homemaker answered the door bell one morning, and was greeted by two beggars. A bit surprised, she asked them:
"Why do you work in a team?"
"Well, you see," answered one of them, "I have sold this street to this man, and I am accompanying him for the first time, to introduce him to my best clients."

Selling is not Easy

Door-To-Door Selling

A young fellow about 12 years old went into the bank, opened a savings account and deposited $75. The banker, being friendly and interested in the boy, said:
"That's a pretty big deposit. How did you earn it?"
"Selling Christmas cards," - replied the little boy.
"You did real well," the banker said. "You must have sold cards to a lot of people in your neighborhood."
"No, sir," said the boy. "One family bought them all. Their dog bit me."

10. Pricing

Price is the amount of money a buyer pays to obtain a product or a service. Price has many different names: fee, fare, rent, tuition, interest, etc. Setting the right price is crucial to a profitable business. Some relevant issues are:

1. How to set profitable prices
2. Should the price be fixed
3. Who should get a price discount

Sellers Estimate Costs
to Determine a Profitable Price

Extra Charges

Solomon had been going through his accounts.
"Did you send a bill to Mr. Brown?" he asked his son.
"Yes, dad," came the reply.
"And did you add an extra dollar on before you sent it?"
"Yes, dad. I added $1.29."
"H'm! What's the twenty-nine cents for?"
"To cover our postage when we reply to his letters complaining of overcharge."

Cost-Plus Pricing

Customer: "What! Six hundred dollars for that antique desk? Last week my neighbor bought the same desk from you for five hundred dollars!"
Store owner: "Sorry, but since then the cost of labor and materials has gone up!"

Paying for Labor (Spain)

"How is it possible that an egg costs six pesetas? Soon we'll not be able to eat tortillas!" protested a lady at the grocer's.
"Six pesetas is cheap!" answered the grocer. "You have to realize that a chicken needs to work a full day to produce an egg!"

Pricing By Location (Russia)

In a small town there was a water-carrier, Mishka, who carried and sold water from the well. When he carried water to a house located close to the well, he used to charge two rubles. On the other hand, when he had to carry the water for a long distance he charged only one ruble. He explained the reason for his pricing system:
"When it's a short distance I don't have time to rest and it is tough on me. But when I carry the water to a distant house I rest several times on the road, and this makes it a lot easier ..."

Keeping Up with Inflation

A peddler posted himself in front of an office building with a tray of shoe laces. One executive made a habit of giving the peddler a dime every day, but he never accepted the laces. This went on for weeks, until one day the peddler, upon receiving the dime, tapped his departing benefactor on the back and complained:
"I don't like to bring this up, sir, but the laces are now fifteen cents!"

Sometimes Price Is Determined
Through Bidding

Bidding

A man bought a parrot at an auction after some very vigorous bidding.
"I hope this bird talks," he said to the auctioneer.
"Does he talk? Who do you think has been bidding against you for the past twenty minutes?"

Pricing Requires Arithmetics

Seven Plus Seven (Chelm, Poland)

Sheina went to the grocery store to buy a herring and a loaf of bread.

"That will be fourteen groschen" said Rabinovich the grocer.

"Fourteen?!" exclaimed Sheina, "I think it's eleven!"

Rabinowich calculated aloud: "The herring costs seven groschen and the loaf of bread costs seven groschen. Together, then, that makes fourteen."

"You don't know how to calculate," said Sheina. "Seven plus seven equals eleven!"

"How come?" laughed the grocer.

"Well, I'll show you," she said. "Listen to this: I had four kids when my husband died. Then I re-married. My second husband already had four kids from his first wife. Afterwards, we had three children together. Which means that each one of us had seven children, and together we have eleven. Now do you believe me?"

Setting the Right Markup

An eager young man sought the advice of an experienced marketing consultant.

"Tell me," he asked, "can I earn a million dollars a year selling flour?"

"Of course," replied the consultant, "all you need to do is buy a million bags of flour at a dollar a bag and sell them for two dollars a bag!"

Dollars and Cents (Egypt)

When Juha was still attending school, one day his arithmetic teacher asked him:
"Let's say your father bought a donkey for twenty dinar and ten piasters, and sold him afterwards for twenty five dinar and six piasters. Did he gain or lose money?"
"He gained in dinars and lost in piasters," was Juha's immediate reply.

Smart Pricing

A good looking young lady entered Goldstein's deli. She was impressed with the owner's shrewdness.
"What is it that makes you so clever?" she asked.
"Herring heads," answered Goldstein immediately. "Eat herring heads, my dear lady, and you'll be smart!"
She bought three heads at 50 cents a piece. A week later she came back and complained that her mental capabilities did not improve.
"You didn't eat enough!" said Goldstein.
This time she bought twenty herring heads and paid ten dollars.
"Listen," she told Goldstein on her next visit, "you sell a whole herring for fifteen cents. Then why do I have to pay fifty cents just for the head?"
"You see," answered Goldstein, extremely satisfied, "you are already smarter!"

One day a kibbutznik took a bus to the big city. He gave
the driver five shekels for a ticket, and, by a mistake, the
driver gave him 95 shekels change. The kibbutznik sat
down. A moment later, the driver realized his mistake,
and asked the kibbutznik:
"How much change did I give you?"
"95 shekels," said the kibbutznik.
"And how much did you originally give me?"
"5 shekels."
"Didn't you realize it was a mistake?" asked the driver.
"No," came the reply. "Do you think I know your prices?"

Sometimes Price Is Influenced by Psychological Factors

Value Is in the Eyes of the Beholder

A woman entered a butcher shop and saw two trays of
meat in the showcase. Upon close examination, she
decided that both trays of meat looked alike to her.
"How much is this meat?" she asked, pointing to one of the
cases.
"Fifty cents a pound," replied the old butcher.
"And that?" she asked, pointing to the other tray.
"One dollar a pound," was the reply.
"What's the difference?"
"No difference; some people like to pay fifty cents a
pound, and others like to pay a dollar!"

When There Is No Competition Sellers Set High Prices

Captive Pricing

A Chicago tourist visited Israel's Negev desert. A Bedouin native offered the visitors a short ride on his camel.
"How much?" asked the Chicagoan.
"One shekel to go up on the camel and have a photo taken."
"Is that all?"
"Not quite," I charge five shekels to get off!"

Customers Believe That
"You Get What You Pay For"

$10 And Up!

"I've solved the mystery of what a hotel means when it advertises 'rooms $10 and up.'"
"Oh yeah, what is it?"
"You get one of the ten-dollar rooms and then you're up all night!"

Some Sellers Sell Two Products
For One Price

Hot Dogs and Mustard (Bulgaria)

A Gabrovonian entered a butcher shop and asked for a pound of hot dogs. The shopkeeper gave him the hot dogs and a small tube of mustard and said:
"That will be a hundred stotinki."
"But I did not ask for mustard," he objected.
"The mustard comes free of charge with the hot dogs," said the shopkeeper.
"Then I shall have only the mustard."

Economy Ticket (Bulgaria)

Old Gregory from Gabrovo wanted to take a train to Sofia.
"Three leva for you and six for your luggage," the ticket-
collector told him.

Old Gregory untied the bundle and said to his son:
"Get out, Pencho! You cost more as a bundle!"

Two for Five Cents

Mrs. Blatt was shopping for cucumbers at the farmers'
market.
"How much are they?" she asked a farmer.
"Two for five cents."

She hesitated, picked one up, and asked again:
"How much is this one?"
"Three cents."

She put it back, picked up the other one, and said,
smiling:
"Fine. I'll take this one for two cents."

Tips Inflate Prices

Doctor's Fee

A successful physician attended a sick child. A few days
later the grateful mother called at his office. After
thanking him for his good service, she handed him a purse
and said:

"I hope you will accept this. I myself have embroidered it."

The doctor replied very coldly to the effect that the fees of a physician must be paid in money, not merely in gratitude, and added:

"Presents maintain friendship. They do not maintain a family."

"What is your fee?" the woman inquired.

"One hundred dollars," was the answer.

The woman opened the purse, and took from it five $100 bills. She put back four, handed one to the physician, and walked out.

Some Sellers
Offer Quantity Discounts

Quantity Discounts (Bulgaria)

A Gabrovonian visited a doctor who used to charge two leva for the first visit and one lev for subsequent ones. Said the Gabrovonian to the doctor:

"The first time I came to see you, you prescribed some medicine, but it didn't do me any good."

The doctor, realizing what the patient was up to, examined him nonetheless, and then said:

"You must continue taking the drug that I prescribed for you the first time."

"As far as I remember, I paid you last time for this advice," said the Gabrovonian, and walked out.

Price Quote

Two salespeople arrived at a hotel. The receptionist showed them an old, dark and shabby room.
"And how much for this pigsty?" asked one of the men.
"Twenty dollars for one pig and twenty-five for two!"

Two-for-a-Quarter

"How much are the cigars?" asked a customer.
"Two for a quarter," said the girl behind the counter.
"I'll take one."
"That'll be fifteen cents."

The customer paid and left. A man who had overheard the transaction came up to the counter.
"Here's a dime," he said. "Give me the other one."

Sellers Mark Down Prices When Sales Are Slow

Price Markdowns

"I hear your store was robbed last night. Lose much?"
"Sure. But it would have been worse if the burglars had got in the night before. You see, yesterday I just finished marking down everything twenty-five percent."

•

Price Can Be Determined
Through Bargaining

Bargaining

An old Texan farmer was riding his mule near the market.
"How much will you sell it to me for?" someone asked.
"I'll sell it to you for a hundred dollars."
"I'm ready to give you five."
"Well, man, I don't want ninety five dollars to ruin our deal. Let it be as you want. Give me five dollars and take the mule!"

Fixed Prices (Russia)

Mendelovich entered a clothing store and saw a nice coat.
"Listen," he said to the owner, "I have to tell you I don't like to bargain. I always pay whatever I'm asked to pay. That's why I'd like you to give me your lowest price for this coat."
Replied the owner:
"In this store it's not appropriate to even talk about such things. My prices are fixed."
"Well," said Mendelovich, "what's the price of this coat?"
"How shall I put it," replied the owner, "I'll not ask you to pay thirty rubles for it, neither twenty five nor twenty rubles. But less than eighteen rubles I cannot quote you."
"And I'll not pay you three rubles, neither four nor five rubles. But more than ten rubles you'll not get!"
    The owner called his salesclerk:
"Volodya! Wrap this coat for the gentleman!"

A Pickle for a Nickel

Mrs. Kleinman went to the market, reached into the pickle barrel and took out a large, fat pickle.

"How much is this pickle?" she asked.

"A nickel," replied Harry the grocer.

"What! A nickel a pickle?" she shouted, outraged.

She tossed the pickle back, plunged her hand deep into the brine and fished up a small pickle.

"Nu, (well), how much is this small pickele?"

"That pickele," answered Harry, "costs only a small nickele!"

You Get What You Pay For

An American tourist was walking with his wife in Paris. They found a perfume shop, the wife went in and he waited outside. A street walker came along and said in English:

"Like to come home with me, Cheri?"

"How much?" ask the tourist.

"Ten hundred francs!" came the answer.

"Five hundred!" offered the man.

"Merde!" whispered the girl and walked away.

A little later the man's wife came out of the shop and they continued their walk. On the corner, there she was, the same streetwalker. She took one look at the couple and said:

"You see? that's what you get for five hundred francs!"

A Mistake in Pricing (Bulgaria)

Passing through Gabrovo, a villager stopped in front of a shop to buy souvenirs. He chose a few items, asked for the price, paid it without bargaining and went away.

The shopkeeper was surprised that the buyer did not bargain for better prices, so he concluded that he could have charged more for the souvenirs. Furiously he ran after the customer, shouting:
"Hey, mister, give me back my goods! ... I don't want your money!"

Half the Price (China)

When a stranger in Soochow was about to go shopping, his friends gave him a piece of advice:
"The Soochow merchants usually try to double the going price, so always offer half of what they are asking."

The next morning the stranger entered a silk-and-satin store. For any piece of goods he offered half of what was asked.

Finally, the shopkeeper grew very angry, and said sarcastically:
"How about this small store making you a present of two bolts of choice silk?"
"Oh, my! No!" the stranger replied, bowing; "this humble servant will accept only one!"

Doctor's Charge

A businessman went to a medical specialist, had a check up, and received a bill for $150.
"Your fee is entirely out of line," he complained to the doctor. "I cannot afford to pay you that amount."
"All right," said the doctor, "make it $100."
"That is still too much. I have a wife and five kids to feed."
"Okay," said the doctor, "make it $50."
This went on until the fee was down to $5.
"Look," said the specialist, "you know I'm a leading specialist and have to charge high prices. Why did you come to me in the first place?"
"Where my health is concerned," answered the businessman, "I never spare money."

Take It or Leave It

Larry entered a pawnshop.
"How much will you pay for this?" he asked, pointing at a used coat.
"Four schilling" replied the owner.
"But this coat is worth at least ten."
"Four schilling or nothing," replied the owner.
"Well," said Larry throwing the money on the counter, "I'll buy it from you. It was hanging outside your store..."

A Real Bargain (Spain)

A man entered a clothing store and pointed at a raincoat:
"How much is it?" he asked.
"Two hundred pesetas, sir!" answered the sales clerk.
"That's too much," the man said. "What can you offer me
for less money?"
"Rain, sir."

Bargaining for a Deal (Arabic fable)

One morning Juha woke up with a terrible toothache. He
went to an amateur, who checked his mouth and said he
had to pull out one rotten tooth.
"How much will you charge me?" asked Juha.
"Three hens," he replied.
"It's too expensive."
"Well, that's my price."
Juha returned home and tried to pull this tooth out
on his own, with pliers. It did not work. Then he took a
thin string, tied one end around the tooth and the other end
he tied to his donkey. Then he pricked the donkey's
behind with a sharp stick. The donkey charged forward,
the string tore off, and the donkey ran away...
All that night Juha could not fall asleep because of
this toothache. Early the next morning he returned to the
amateur, gave him three hens and said:
"Go ahead, pull it out!"
The guy used his pliers, pulled it hard, and took out
the tooth, roots and everything.
Said Juha:
"Three hens for a minute's work? Aren't you ashamed?
How about pulling out another one?"

Some Sellers Set Higher Prices to Certain Consumers

What the Market Will Bear (Turkey)

His Imperial Majesty arrived unexpectedly at the teahouse where Nasrudin had been left in charge.

The Emperor ordered an omelette for himself and for the people who were with him.

"We shall now continue with the hunt," he told the Mulla, after they finished eating, "so tell me what I owe you."

"For you and your five companions, your Highness, the omelettes will be a thousand gold pieces."

The Emperor raised his eyebrows in disbelief.

"Eggs must be very costly here. Are they that scarce?"

"It's not the eggs which are scarce here, Majesty. It's the visits of kings!"

Pricing Eye Glasses

The proprietor of a highly successful optical shop was instructing his son.

"Son," he said, "after you have fitted the glasses, and the customer asks what the charge will be, you say: 'the charge is $10.00.' Then pause and wait to see if he flinches. If he does not flinch you then say, 'for the frames. The lenses will be another $10.00.' Then you pause again, this time only slightly, and watch for the flinch. If the customer does not flinch this time, you say, firmly: 'Each.'"

Pricing By the Diet (Bulgaria)

A doctor was asked by a patient:
"Why do you always ask your patients about their diet?"
"It helps me determine the fee," answered the doctor.

The Right Price

One morning a strange man knocked on the farm's front door and a girl opened it.
"I'd like to talk with your father," said the man.
"Dad is in the field right now, but I'm familiar with all his business and you can talk with me too. If you want an ox, the price is $500. If you want a horse - the price is $700. If you want a pig - the price is $300."
"Oh, no, young lady. It's not that. It's concerning your brother, Johnny. He is dating my daughter and I thought it would be good if we parents knew each other." At this point the girl interrupted and said:
"Well, if so, you'd better see Daddy. I don't know how much he asks for Johnny."

No Free Lunch (Bulgaria)

"Doctor, am I glad I met you!" said a Gabrovonian to his doctor, whom he met in the street; "tell me, what do you do when you have a cold in the head?"
"I sneeze," replied the doctor, who was also from Gabrovo.

Room Charge (Bulgaria)

A Gabrovonian went to a hotel that did not have an elevator.

"How much do you charge for a night's lodging?" he asked.

"Ten leva for the first floor, eight for the second, six for the third, and four for the fourth."

The Gabrovonian stopped to think for a moment and then was preparing to walk away.

"What's the matter?" asked the hotel keeper.

"Your hotel, sir, is not high enough."

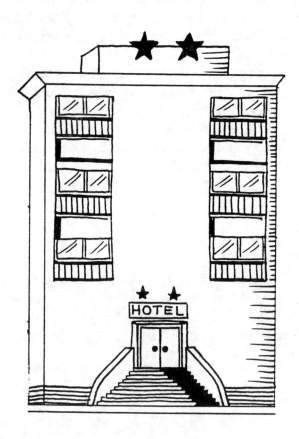

11. Promotion Strategies

Promotions are communications to inform buyers about products and encourage them to buy. Advertising, sales promotions (such as coupons, rebates and free gifts), personal selling, and public relations, are all classified as promotions. Some promotional decision areas are:

1. When, where, and what to advertise and promote
2. What kinds of incentives to offer
3. How to plan and make good sales presentations
4. How to build and maintain a good sales force

Why Advertise?

The Power of Advertising

At a conference of advertisers, one of the speakers stated: "The fish lays thousands and thousands of eggs, but the fish stays mute. The chicken on the other hand makes lots and lots of noise with every one egg she lays. Who gets more attention? the chicken, of course! And that's the power of advertising!"

Advertising Reminds Consumers About the Product

A Reminder

The following notice was sent to a magazine subscriber two years after his subscription had expired:
"Dear subscriber:
I am sorry to let you know that after many attempts to obtain your subscription renewal, computer records indicate that you have not yet replied affirmatively. Therefore, the publisher has issued instructions that you continue to be contacted until you renew your subscription."

Advertisers Decide Who
Will Deliver the Message

Selling Pickles (Egypt)

Juha decided to start a business selling pickles. He
acquired a few jars of pickles, loaded them on his donkey,
and started out in the narrow streets of his town, shouting:
"Pickles, pickles!"
But each time he shouted, "Pickles, pickles", his donkey
would bray loudly and make his voice inaudible. Finally
Juha lost his temper and yelled angrily at his donkey:
"Who is selling the pickles, you or me?"

Is Advertising Always Beneficial?

Ruined Reputation

"I'm ruined! Last night my factory was broken in!"
"Did they take a lot?"
"They did not take anything, but now they are going to tell everybody that my cash register is empty!"

Poor Communication Results in Ineffective Marketing

Communication and Business

Isaac, the owner of several department stores, was sitting in his office when the telephone rang. Saul, his buyer, was on the line:
"Listen carefully, I've got to read you an important telegram from our gloves supplier.
"Go ahead and read it," said Isaac.
"Wait a second. The secretary is here; she'll read it."
     The secretary began: "We have a great sale ... stop ... Ladies' gloves ... stop ... Assorted colors ... stop ... Twenty five percent discount ... stop ... "
"Saul!" roared Isaac over the telephone, "leave the girl alone and let her read the telegram. This is business!"

Achieving Effective Promotion Through Word of Mouth

Referrals

Mrs. Taylor thought the doctor was overcharging for seeing her son through a siege of the measles.

"Don't forget," the doctor reminded her, "that I visited your son eleven times."

"But don't you forget," she countered, "my son infected the whole school."

Doing Business! (Egypt)

A guy bumped into Juha in the marketplace and told him: "Juha, I saw a boy carrying on his head a tray with two roasted chickens!"

"Well," said Juha, "and what do I care? It's none of my business!"

"It was for you!"

"If so," answered Juha, "it's none of YOUR business!"

Gone Home

A salesman of tombstones and a recent widow were discussing the epitaph to be inscribed on her late husband's gravestone.

"How would a simple 'Gone Home' do?" asked the salesman.

"I think that would suit nicely," replied the widow, whose husband was a salesman as well. "It was always the last place he ever thought of going."

Humor Can Enhance Marketing

Different Jokes to Different Folks

An American marketing manager was invited to give a sales presentation to a group of Japanese executives. He started his speech with a joke and an interpreter translated the joke into Japanese. When he finished, everybody was laughing loudly.

After the talk, the American approached the interpreter and said:

"They really enjoyed my joke, didn't they?"

"Well," said the interpreter, "when I translated the joke nobody responded so I continued and said: 'Our guest has just told a joke. Please laugh now ...'"

‎ertisers Use Different Vehicles
for Their Messages

Hot Air Balloon

An advertising agent went on a hot air balloon, which carried a large advertisement for a company his agency represented. After a few minutes, the agent noticed that he forgot his compass. Then he saw a man down on the ground.
"Where am I?" the guy shouted.
"In a hot air balloon," came the answer.
"You are an accountant, right?"
"How do you know?"
"I know because you've given me information which is 100% accurate and 100% worthless."

Catalogue Selling

A thriving industrial plant in Mexico employed twenty local women. One day the women did not show up to work. The owner offered them a higher pay and shorter hours. The women responded that they earned all they needed for the next six months at least. Why work any more? The boss, after much worry, finally hit upon a solution. He sent each of them a thousand-page Chicago mail order catalogue. The following Monday they were all back at their work stations.

Why Advertise?

In order to prove he was very successful immediately from the start, Mark Twain used to tell the following story: As it happened, he first worked as an editor for a newspaper. One day, a few hours before the newspaper was printed, a man came in and wanted to put in an ad promising a prize to the founder of his lost dog.
"And," asked Twain, "do you think I put this ad in the newspaper? no way! I went out, found the dog just before the newspaper came out, and thus I won the prize!"

Designing a Good Ad

While Supply Lasts (France)

A lady came rushing into a shoe store all out of breath.
"Is it true what I've read in the newspaper? Do you really have five hundred pairs of pumps on sale?"
"Yes, mademoiselle."
"Let me try them on!" she said.

The Perfect Ad

"Sold your house yet?"
"Well, after reading the agent's description we've decided not to sell. It seems to be exactly the home of our dreams!"

Advertising Does Not Always Work (Egypt)

Juha took his cow to the market in order to sell her. But all his announcements regarding her beauty and other qualities did not seem to help, because nobody believed him. One of his friends volunteered to help. He took the cow to the market and started to walk her around, stating her qualities, announcing that she was very strong, and also that she was pregnant, in her fourth month. Immediately some people gathered around him, and the cow was sold at a higher price than expected by Juha.

A few days later some matchmakers came to Juha's house in order to see his daughter and suggest a good match for her. Juha's wife demanded that he leave the house on the spot so that he would not see the matchmakers, nor be seen by them.

"All right," said Juha. "But don't tell them anything about our daughter. Let them see her and that's all. And let me talk with them behind the curtains later."

After the matchmakers saw the beautifully dressed girl and started bargaining about the dowry, Juha's wife sent them to talk with him.

"My dear ladies," said Juha, "no point in all this talking. After all, this is my daughter and I cannot exaggerate her qualities, personality and good nature. One thing I can vouch for her: this daughter of mine is very strong, and pregnant in her fourth month!"

Hearing this, the matchmakers rushed out of the house, running as fast as they could...

Advertisers Often Overstate
the Benefits of Products

Truth in Advertising

Friend: "Did you ever run up against a mathematical problem that baffled you?"

Famous mathematician: "Yes, indeed. I could never figure out how, according to the ads, seventy-five percent of the dentists recommend one brand of toothpaste, and eighty-five percent recommend another brand."

Misleading Advertising (Poland)

A sign in front of a store said: "WE SELL SILK CLOTHES." A customer entered and asked for a silk blouse for his wife.

"Where shall I get a silk blouse from?" asked the owner, quite perplexed. "We carry only used merchandise!"

"But if that's so, why do you have this sign in front of your store?" asked the confused customer.

"That sign is second-hand too and it's also for sale!"

Pawnshop Advertising

Sign in the window of a pawnshop:
"Come in! Don't be shy!
Borrow your way out of debt!"

Spelling - and Selling

A sign in a store window read: "Fishing Tickle."
Noticing the error, a customer asked:
"Hasn't anyone told you about this before?"
"Yes," replied the dealer, "many have dropped in to tell
me, and they always end up buying something."

How to Sell a Book (France)

The following ad appeared in a local newspaper in Nice,
France:
"Millionaire, young, good-looking man, wishes to marry a
girl like the heroine in M's novel."
Within 24 hours M's novel was sold out.

The Right Advertising Idea

A large department store put out a big sign: "The biggest sale in our history!"

The owner of the small shop next to the department store decided he could not compete with that one, so he put up a sign that said: "Entrance to the sale!"

Product Display

Sam walked into a Jewish deli, sat down and ordered a pastrami sandwich. When his meal arrived, he angrily called the owner over and said:

"Listen, Mr. Kluger, I ordered this same kind of sandwich yesterday and it had three times as much meat!"

"Yesterday," replied Kluger, "you were sitting at the window!"

Window Display (England)

A stylish lady entered a shop and pointed out a hat in the window:
"That red one with the feathers and berries," she said, "could you take it out of the window for me?"
"Certainly, madam," the clerk agreed. "I would be happy to."
"Thank you so much," said the lady as she moved toward the exit, "the awful thing upsets me very much as I pass by!"

Sales Promotions Are Incentives to Encourage Buying

Soap Coupons

A woman was showing a friend the kitchen of her house.
"We clipped soap coupons, and with the savings we finished the kitchen," she said.
"With soap coupons!" the friend exclaimed. "What about the other rooms?"
"Oh, those are filled with soap!"

Promotion and Luck

A credit card company offered an accident insurance policy to its new card subscribers. Their advertisement said:

"T. S. Morgan subscribed to our credit card and was given a free accident policy. On his way home from work, he fell down and broke his arm, jaw, and both legs. The accident policy paid him $5,000. You may be the lucky one tomorrow!"

Marketers Offer Free Samples

Free Samples (Arabic)

An Arab was reclining under a shade of a carob tree, preparing for a good rest. Close to him, a group of kids were playing, running around and making lots of noise. It really started to bother him and he did not know what to do. Finally he had an idea.

"Kids," he said, "in the next village they are giving free samples of watermelons!"

In a minute - there was no one to disturb him anymore. All the kids disappeared.

And the Arab was laying peacefully under the tree for a few minutes until it dawned on him:

"Well," he said to himself, "if they are giving away watermelons, what am I doing here?"

Salespeople Must be Familiar with their Products

Pre-Sale Preparation

To help a new salesman become familiar with the company's product, the sales manager suggested he demonstrate it to his wife. The next morning the manager asked:

"How did the presentation go?"

"I did what you told me," he said, "and when I finished, I asked my wife: 'Would you buy it?' She said: 'Yes!' When I asked her why, she replied, 'Because I love you!'"

Salespeople Must Understand What Their Customers Need

A Perfect Suit

A man entered a clothing store to buy a suit. The salesman asked him for his name, age, profession, education, hobbies, political party, and his wife's maiden name.

"Why do you need all this information?" the customer asked.

"Sir, this is not just an ordinary tailor shop," the salesman said. To find you a suit that is exactly right for you, we need to study your personality, background and your surroundings. We order from Australia the kind of sheep your character and mood require. We ship that particular blend of wool to London to be combed and sponged according to a special formula. Then the wool is woven in a region of Scotland where the climate matches your temperament. After much careful thought and study, the suit is made and..."

"Wait a minute," the customer said. "I need this suit tomorrow night for my nephew's wedding."

"Don't worry," the salesman said. "You'll have it!"

Prospecting Means Selecting Potential Buyers

Selling a Car to the Joneses

Sales Manager: "I think it's a good time to approach the Joneses and offer them a new car."
Salesman: "What makes you think so?"
Sales Manager: "Their neighbors got a new one."

Memory-Training

Jack Smith ran into John Corcoran at a trade show in New York City.
Jack: "Well, if it isn't John Corcoran, the salesman I met up in Maine one rainy night six years ago at the Moose River Junction railway station!"
John: "Good bye, sir."
Jack: "Aren't you going to try and sell me something?"
John: "No sir. I sell memory-training courses!"

Going Fishing (France)

A newly hired salesperson, was showing fishing equipment to a customer in a department store in Paris:
"Have a look. With this rod you will attract fish within a huge radius! Naturally I'll give you thirty meters of line, with five or six hooks. And, of course, you are going to need a stool to sit on, right?"

"Right," replied the customer.

"Then let's move to the next department. Look! here is a small, handcrafted stool. It's exactly your size! And what about a basket? You're going to need something to put the fish in! Here's one that will carry up to ten kilos. This is the last one I have! And by the way, where do you plan to go fishing? Personally, I'd advise you to go to the ocean. And you'd better have a boat. I don't mean a yacht, you know. Just a small boat will do. Come with me to the basement. Here's a boat recommended by the fishermen's union. And if you wish, we can install a 3 horse-power motor on it. I think you might find it handy on the high-seas.

Now tell me, how will you get to the beach?"
"By train," replied the man.
"That's not very practical. The ideal way is to be in control, coming and going whenever you wish. Follow me to the automobile department. Look at this car model. Fantastic. You even have special cables here on top to help secure all your fishing gear. Certainly, you may pay by installments! And I suppose you would like a car radio as well? You definitely need something to entertain you on the road! Well now, it looks like we're all settled. Everything will be delivered to you tomorrow morning. It's been a pleasure doing business with you!"

The store's manager who witnessed everything, approached the salesperson full of admiration and said:
"What a talent! this guy came in to buy a fishing rod and you sold him a stool, a basket, a boat, a car..."
"Oh," said the salesperson, "he didn't come in to buy a fishing rod. I saw him at the pharmacy department asking for sanitary napkins for his wife, and so I said to him: 'Since your wife is out of commission, you ought to go fishing...'"

Salespeople Prepare
Sales Presentations

Selling a Life Insurance Policy

Insurance agent: "Sir, if you pay me $20 a month, you will not die. I guarantee it."
Customer: "That's impossible. I don't believe it."
Insurance agent: "I'm absolutely sure about it; and to prove it to you, I am willing to put my money where my mouth is. Pay me $20 a month, and if you die, I will pay your wife $100,000 on the spot!"

Keeping Sales-Presentations Short

A group of salespeople attended a sales conference. The organizers decided that in order for everyone to get equal time for the sales-presentation, each salesperson will deliver his sales-pitch standing on one leg. The moment he gets tired will be the signal for the next salesperson to start.

Death Insurance

Solberg, the insurance agent, went to Langer's house.
"Mr. Langer," said Solberg, "how much life insurance are you carrying?"
"Ten thousand dollars."
"How long do you think you can stay dead on that kind of money?"

A Convincing Sales-Pitch

An excellent salesman had a mid-life crisis. He climbed a bridge railing and was about to jump when a policeman appeared:

"Hey!" shouted the officer, "you can't do that!"

"Why not?" challenged the salesman, and went on to argue the point with the policeman. After half an hour they both jumped.

Salespeople Are Ready to Handle Rejections

Handling Rejections

"How is it going?" the veteran sales manager asked a rookie salesperson.

"Rotten. I get nothing but insults every place I call."

"That's funny," the old man remarked. "I've been on the road forty years. I've had doors slammed in my face and my samples dumped in the street. I've been tossed downstairs and been manhandled by janitors, but insults? Never!"

Salespeople Respond to Post-Purchase Concerns

A Shrewd Matchmaker (Chelm, Poland)

Mendel the matchmaker finally found a bride for Zelig, the most naive guy in the village. Three months later Zelig's new wife gave birth to a baby boy. Confused, he rushed to the matchmaker's house.

"Mendel," he said, "my wife, Bluma, just gave birth to a baby boy."

"Wives usually do," said old Mendel. "Congratulations!"

"But we have only been married three months. My mother, may she rest in peace, told me it takes nine months to bear a baby."

Mendel thought for a moment and asked:

"How long have you been married?"

"Three months."

"How long has your wife been living with you?"

"Three months."

"And how long have you been living together?"

"Also three months."

"Now add up: three months plus three months plus three months. What do you get?"

"Nine months."

"See," said Mendel, "your mother was right!"

Honest Salespeople Reveal
Product Disadvantages

An Honest Agent

"There are advantages and disadvantages about this property," said the honest real estate agent. "To the north is the sewage treatment facility, to the east horse stables, to the south a fish and chip shop, and to the west a bakery. Those are the disadvantages."
"What are the advantages?"
"You can always tell which way the wind is blowing."

Blue Fabric (France)

A customer entered a store:
"I need some blue fabric."
"Yes, monsieur, I'm going to show it to you right away," said the sales clerk, and went to the storage room. He returned with a bolt of green cloth.
"Splendid fabric, isn't it?" said the clerk. "Touch it, please!"
"But I've told you I need blue fabric!" protested the customer.
"Blue? Oh, yes. Blue. I'm going to bring you exactly what you need," said the clerk, and went away again. This time he returned with some magnificent plaid material.
"Have a look at this material. Top of the line!"
"For crying out loud!" shouted the customer. "Didn't you get it? I need blue!"
"Oh, monsieur. If it's blue fabric that you need, I mean real blue, well, this I don't have!"

Some Salespeople use
Hard-Sell Techniques

Selling Suits

A man entered a store to buy a suit. One of the store owners tried every suit but one on the customer. Each time the fellow put on a suit, the owner would turn him around and around so he could view himself in the mirror. Finally, the other owner took over, showed the customer one suit, and made a sale.

"You see how easy it was," he admonished. "I did it on the first try!"

"I know," shrugged his partner, "but who made him dizzy?"

Selling a House

Customer: "I like the house, but the inside walls are so thin that the neighbor is going to hear everything I say!"

Builder: "I have a suggestion for you. Try the following experiment. Enter the next room and I'll whistle. If you hear the whistle, it means that I have to build thicker walls."

They performed the experiment. The customer then said:

"I have not heard anything, but ..."

Builder: "You want to say I haven't whistled at all. Well then, let's reverse rolls: I'll go in the next room, and you whistle!"

Scaring Technique

A life insurance agent visited a prospective client.
"Look," the agent said, "with a wife and three kids you cannot afford not to have life insurance. I recommend a policy of $200,000."
The prospective client did not respond.
"What if I tell you," continued the agent, "that the policy will cost you only $1 per day?"
The prospective client did not respond.
"Listen," said the agent, "you don't have to give me an answer today. Sleep on it tonight, and if you get up tomorrow, give me a call!"

Talking Business

Judge to salesman: "You had a gun pulled on Mr. Goldstein, yet you didn't pull the trigger. Why?"
Salesman: "Well, judge, when I pointed my pistol at him, he said: 'Tell me, how much do you want for that gun?' How could I kill a man when he was talking business? ..."

Sales Managers Recruit
and Keep Good Salespeople

Selling Smart

The shoe store owner was interviewing a salesperson.
"Suppose you try to fit a lady with a pair of shoes and she says: 'Don't you think one of my feet is bigger than the other?' What would you tell her?"
"I would say: 'On the contrary, madam, one is smaller than the other.'"
"You're hired!"

An Ambitious Salesman (Turkey)

Nasrudin was being interviewed for a sales job.
Sales manager: "We like ambitious men here."
Nasrudin: "All right, I would like to have YOUR job."
"What, are you mad?" shouted the sales manager.
"Is that a requirement for the job?" asked Nasrudin.

Mistreating Customers

A salesman was fired because he mistreated a customer A few days later the company's sales manager saw the ex-salesman on the street wearing a policeman's uniform.
"I see you've joined the force, Jones," said the manager.
"Yes," replied Jones. "This is the job I've been looking for all my life. On this job the customer is always wrong."

A Sales Manager
Motivates His Salespeople

A Sales Contest

A sales manager summoned all his salesmen for a special sales meeting.
"Gentlemen," he said, "today, we're announcing a big sales contest. It will start tomorrow morning and will run for eight weeks."
The salesmen were excited, and one of the men on the front row asked:
"What does the winner get?"
"He gets to keep his job," replied the sales manager.

Delegating Responsibilities

The sales manager called Jim and told him he was going to increase his responsibilities. "Starting today," he said to the excited salesperson, "you'll be responsible for everything that goes wrong!"

An Absent-Minded Salesperson

"Marvin is so forgetful," complained a sales manager to his secretary; "I asked him to pick me up a pack of cigarettes on his way back from lunch, but I'm not even sure he'll remember to come back himself."

A few minutes later Marvin dashed into the office, shouting:

"What a break, boss! At lunch, I met old man Hess, who hasn't bought a penny's worth from us in five years and before we parted I talked him into a half-a-million-dollar order!"

"What did I tell you?" sighed the sales manager, "he forgot the cigarettes!"

Happy Birthday (France)

A salesperson was invited by his sales manager to her home on his birthday. Some time later he told one of his friends about it:

"She offered me a martini with salted almonds, she put on some soft music and then she said to me: 'I'm going to give you a nice surprise. I'll go to my room now, and I want you to join me in five minutes.'"

"Fabulous!" said the friend. "Weren't you happy?"

"Wait a minute! Listen carefully now. When I entered her room, I found all the people from the office there cheering: 'Surprise! happy birthday!'"

"Well, I hope at least you took it like a good sport."

"Easy for you to say! I was completely naked!"

Sales Force Compensation

Salesman: "Sir, my wife said I should ask for a raise."
Sales manager: "I'll ask my wife if I may give you one."

What Did He Buy?

Manager: "Why didn't that man buy anything? What did he want to see?"
Pretty saleslady: "Me, tomorrow night."

Salespeople Travel all the Time

A Salesperson's Day (Spain)

"Doctor," complained the salesperson, "I am really desperate. I wake up every morning with the rooster's call. I work like a horse. I eat like a lion. At night I go to bed about the same time as the birds, and I sleep like a marmot. However, I don't feel well. What should I do?"
"I'll refer you to a vet," replied the doctor.

Who Does the Selling

A businessman was on the road three months already. Every week he used to send a telegram to his wife: "I cannot come home. Still buying." The wife was patient, but after four such telegrams she decided to react. She telegraphed him the following: "Come home - or else I start selling."

Sharing a Sales Territory (Poland)

In a court of law, the judge asked Mendel Zelikowitch, a salesman, about his business.
"What can I tell you, your honor? I move around!" answered Mendel.
The judge moved around Mendel and asked:
"Well, I'm moving around too. Can I make my living this way?"
"Let me move around you," said Mendel. "This way both of us will make a living!"

Travel Expenses

Sales Manager: "What's this big item on your expense-account?"
Travelling salesman: "Oh, that's the bill for my hotel."
Sales Manager: "Well, don't buy any more hotels!"

12. Marketing Ethics

Marketers are sometimes blamed for using practices that are unfair, immoral, or dishonest.

Marketing People
Should Not Take Bribe

The Ethical Official (Russia)

A Russian official visited a car factory. The Vice President Marketing went out of his way to show him around and at the end of the tour offered him a free car. "Oh no," refused the official, "I cannot accept it."
"Well, then I'll sell it to you for five rubles."
The official handed him a bill of ten rubles and said:
"In that case, I'll have two."

Handling Bribes

An old judge opened court with the following announcement:
"Gents, I have in hand a check, a bribe you could call it, I guess, from the plaintiff for $10,000 and another from the defendant for $15,000. I propose to return $5,000 to the defendant, and then we will decide the case strictly on its merits."

Overstating Product Performance

Misrepresentation (Egypt)

A drug dealer approached Juha in an alley. He told Juha that hashish is an intoxicating drug, pleasing and dazing the senses, in short - it's a worthwhile adventure to undertake! Juha, being extremely tempted to try it out, bought some. After taking it, he went into the public bath. Sitting there, he began to notice that the hashish was not working the way he was promised it would.

He immediately decided to go to the man he bought the hashish from and reproach him for selling him fake hashish. He went out of the public bath wearing nothing but his birthday suit, and started jumping around and advancing in dance steps. People stopped him and asked him what was the reason for his strange behavior.

"I'm going to rebuke the man who sold me fake hashish. It didn't influence me at all, as you can see for yourselves!"

Some Buyers Do Not Make Payments on Time

Bad Credit (Russia)

Kaplan, a grocery store owner, and Rabinovich, one of his customers, went to see the rabbi.

"Rabbi," pleaded Kaplan, "this man owes me five hundred rubles and he does not want to pay."

"Liar," said Rabinovich, "I told you I can't pay before the end of this month!"

"Rabbi," said Kaplan in anger, "those were his exact words last month!"

"Well," said Rabinovich, "didn't I keep my word?"

Who Should Get Credit (Chelm, Poland)

The melamed (teacher) and the rabbi of Chelm met in a coffee house and discussed ways to improve the town's welfare. Said the melamed:

"There is one thing that depresses me the most. The rich, who have more money than they need, can buy on credit. But the poor, who don't have two coins to their name, have to pay cash for everything. Do you call that fair?"

"I don't see how it could be any other way," answered the rabbi.

"But it's only common sense that it should be the other way around," insisted the melamed; "the rich should pay cash, and the poor should be able to buy on credit."

"I admire your idealistic nature," said the rabbi, "but a merchant who extends credit to the poor instead of the rich

will soon become a poor man himself."
"So what?" retorted the melamed, "then he'd be able to buy on credit, too!"

Some Traders Try to Outsmart Their Partners

The Wine Maker's Secret (Poland)

In a little village in Poland, there once lived a wine maker. There was an abundance of water, and the wine maker believed that too much wine was unhealthy. He worried that people would get drunk as rats, God forbid...
    Then the day came when it was time for him to die. Thinking about heaven and hell, he summoned his sons to his bed, and said:
"Listen to me, children, and listen well. Wine can be made out of grapes too..."

Collecting The Check (Bulgaria)

A waiter at a Gabrovo restaurant asked another:
"Why don't you turn that fellow out? You keep on waking him up and he falls asleep at the table again and again."
"Why should I? Every time I wake him up he asks for his check, and every time he pays it without a fuss!"

Who Needs Cash in Heaven? (Argentina)

Dying, Isaac summoned his three sons to his bed, and in a weak voice, almost whispering, he said to them:
"As I do not know what happens in the world I am about to enter, I beg each one of you to set aside fifty thousand pesos as an advance payment for my first expenses there, in case it turns out to be necessary."

A few moments later, Isaac died. Before the casket was closed, the eldest son put the promised money inside. The second son did the same. When it came the turn of the youngest, he took out his brothers' one hundred thousand pesos and left a check for one hundred fifty thousand made out to the order of the deceased.

Examples of Dishonest Marketing

Relativity

Ferguson had acquired a reputation as such a dishonest dealer that when he died nobody in town would agree to say the eulogy. The priest had no choice but to handle it himself. This is the eulogy he delivered:
"Joseph Ferguson, may you rest in peace. In comparison to your father you were a saint!"

Doing Business the Honest Way (Argentina)

Nathan and Shmuel discussed business over lunch. Said Shmuel:
"There are thousands of methods to make a fortune. But to do it honestly - there is only one way."
"And which one is that?" asked Nathan, curiously.
"Aha!" exclaimed Shmuel maliciously, "I've suspected that you do not know it ..."

A Dishonest Store Clerk

The customer to the store owner:
"Why did you let your daughter marry your store clerk? Didn't you say you don't trust him?"
"I still don't trust him," answered the owner, "but then I thought if he steals from me, at least the money will go to my daughter!"

Why Steal?

Bob got caught in a store stealing a lap-top computer.
"Why did you have to steal it?" asked his wife, "Couldn't you just buy one and not pay for it?"

Where is the Meat? (Arabic)

Juha left his butcher store in charge of his helper and went to run some errands. When he returned, he realized that five pounds of the best quality meat were missing. When he demanded an explanation, the helper told him that the cat had eaten the meat.

Juha could not believe his eyes and ears. He seized the cat, and put it on the scales. It weighed five pounds. He held the cat up in the air, and asked his helper:
"If this is the cat, where is the meat? And if this is the meat, where is the cat?"

Index